HOW TO BECOME FINANCIALLY INDEPENDENT STATE BY STATE FORCLOSURE WHOLESALING
(Without Owning Property)

By Mark O. Cheeley

Copyright © 2019 Mark O. Cheeley

ISBN 978-1-949720-40-2

All Rights Reserved.
No part of this publication may be reproduced, distributed, or transmitted in any form or by any means, including photocopying, recording, or other electronic or mechanical methods, without the prior written permission of the author, except the use of brief quotations for the sole purpose of a book review.

Terms of Usage

TERMS OF USAGE

All course material, products and intellectual property modified or unmodified are owned exclusively by MCheeleyPA, D/B/A/ National Short Sale Institute™. No part of this course material may be reproduced or used in any form by any means or resold without express written permission. Once you have paid for and completed the National Foreclosure Short Sale Institute "Certified Expert"SM short sale course you will have membership benefits for One Year from certification. Membership benefits entitle you to use the company initials NFSSI "Certified Expert"SM and logo on your advertising, website, business cards and any other collateral materials that you use to advertise your services. You must maintain your membership annually or all rights will be revoked.

Disclaimer
The contents of this course material include information relating to general principals of real estate that should not be construed as specific instructions for individual transactions. Application of this information in a situation remains the professional responsibility of the licensed real estate professional. MCheeleyPA, D/B/A National Foreclosure Short Sale Institute™ assumes no liability or responsibility for any errors or omissions in such information.

Release of Liability
All course materials, forms and learning systems included in the NFSSI "Certified Expert"SM Short Sale Course are provided as guidelines and examples and must be verified for their accuracy and usability in your market and individual clients on a case by case basis. It is understood and agreed upon that the user of the course materials agree to hold harmless MCheeleyPA, LLC. D/B/A National Foreclosure Short Sale Institute™, its officers, owners, employees and contractors for any issued arising from the usage of these materials.

Course Information
This course is designed to provide accurate and authoritative information regarding the subject matter covered. Any use by a company or individual who has not completed the NFSSI "Certified Expert" course is expressly prohibited. Any mass duplication unmodified or otherwise is expressly prohibited. At no time can any part of the NFSSI "Certified Expert" Short Sale Course manual be duplicated. Additional copies are available for sale from the company. The course materials are sold with the understanding that the author and publisher are not engaged in rendering legal, accounting, or other professional services to any person. If legal advice and / or other expert assistance is required, the service of a competent professional should be sought through the American Bar Association 1-800-285-2221.

Penalty for Copyright Infringement
The owner of a registered copyright can enforce his rights by bringing a civil lawsuit in Federal District Court. In addition, the Federal government itself can act. Criminal actions can be brought by the U.S. Attorney; and Customs and Postal officials may seize and impound infringing articles that are being imported. Recovery of attorney's fees is possible if the suit is successful. The penalties for infringement can be substantial. In civil actions brought by the copyright owner, the court may order forfeiture and/or destruction not only of all infringing articles, but also of any implements used to manufacture the infringing articles. The court may even order seizure and impoundment of such articles prior to trial, and in some cases, without prior notice to the alleged infringer. In addition to obtaining an order stopping the infringement and ordering destruction of infringing articles, the court can order payment of any provable damages, including lost profits. The copyright owner can elect to receive "statutory damages". The minimum amount of statutory damages that can be awarded for copyright infringement is $750; and the maximum is $30,000. If the infringement was willful, the potential statutory damage award is increased to $150,000 for each act of infringement. In addition, attorneys' fees may be awarded. In addition to civil penalties, copyright infringers can be prosecuted under the federal criminal laws. All willful copyright infringement is a criminal offense. The lowest penalty is conviction of a federal misdemeanor, with a prison sentence of up to one year and a fine of up to $5000. More serious penalties are levied against infringers who make multiple copies of a work, or who copy expensive works. It is a felony, punishable by up to five years in prison and a fine of up to $250,000 to willfully infringe copyrights of others by making, during a 180-day period, ten or more copies of a work which have a cumulative value of
$2500 or more. Second and subsequent offenses carry a prison term of up to ten years in addition to the fine. Companies or individuals which willfully infringe can be assessed up to $500,000 in fines.

ACKNOWLEDGEMENTS / COURSE INFORMATION

Acknowledgements

I would like to thank the NFSSI "Certified Expert"℠ Team of professionals for their invaluable expertise, guidance and preparation of the materials contained in the course presented herein.

The National Foreclosure Short Sale Institute™ "Certified Expert" team of seasoned real estate professional realtor's, brokers, agents, attorneys and title companies throughout the United States are working together to provide a safe, ethical solution to avoid pitfalls for homeowners with their short sales and foreclosure problems.

Course Information

This course is designed to provide accurate and authoritative information as to the subject matter covered. It is sold with the understanding that the author and publisher are not engaged in rendering legal, accounting, or other professional services to any person. If legal advice and / or other expert assistance is required, the services of a competent professional should be sought through the American Bar Association 1-800-285-2221.

Upon reproduction of this material you further agree to hold harmless National Foreclosure Short Sale Institute, and its officers, owners, employers and affiliates for any issues arising from the use of this course in any form or by any means, unless otherwise noted, and any use or reproduction is a strictly prohibited without the written permission of MCheeleyPA.

Branding with our logos or initials of any material copied is granted with limited revocable release to you to use as a "Certified Expert"℠ of the National Foreclosure Short Sale Institute.

DISCLAIMER:

This manual has been written to conform with the laws and ethics that pertain to the general real estate guidelines for the 50 United States.

The examples and procedures of legal contracts used in this manual have been approved by the Florida Association of Realtors® and the Florida Bar Association of Florida (FAR / BAR) use only.

Our Role

OUR ROLE

To increase your pipeline of business and to help you soar to new levels of success in the new "Tradition" of short sales.

Our organization keeps you abreast of the current mortgage crisis in the United States.

Homeowners are currently facing financial distress at historic levels, more than at any other time in history of real estate.

Our methods of acceleration due to government programs help you facilitate options for your Seller / Borrower in the event that the new program Home Affordable Foreclosure Alternative (HAFA) should not help your buyer / seller solve their problem.

Exercising our step by step techniques with the Seller / Borrowers package and the Coordinator / Processor Lender / Investor package will set yourself apart from your peers, as you are branding yourself as a National Foreclosure Short Sale Institute™ "Certified Expert" in your marketplace.

As our ongoing continuing support has no limit when it comes to short sales. The new "Tradition" transaction in the real estate market will now reap the rewards of your success.

The National Foreclosure Short Sale Institute™ "Certified Expert" team of seasoned real estate professional realtors, brokers, agents, attorneys, and title companies throughout the United States are working together to provide a safe, ethical solution to avoid the pitfalls for homeowners with their short sales and foreclosure problems.

Our program elevates you for more listings as the marketplace is never ending.

Your success is our success.

Company Profile

COMPANY PROFILE

National Foreclosure Short Sale Institute™   www.NFSSICE.COM

Mark Cheeley, with his team, is traveling the country training thousands of Real Estate professionals on how to help distressed Sellers. Real Estate professionals attend his training course and become a NFSSI "Certified Expert"[SM]. Short sale transactions today are the fastest growing niche in the Real Estate Industry. The National Foreclosure Short Sale Institute™ "Certified Expert" Team of seasoned real estate professional realtor's, brokers, agents, attorneys and title companies throughout the United States are working together to provide a safe, ethical solution to avoid the pitfalls for homeowners with their short sales and foreclosure problems.

In 2007 President and CEO of NFSSI "Certified Expert" Mark Cheeley developed training and marketing material for the Real Estate industry. He produced a comprehensive educational course for the Realtor, Broker and Agent on property owners' options. For the homeowner that is underwater or in financial hardships. Cheeley has a designated website NFSSICE.com that is an informative site for the Real Estate Industry. Cheeley connects homeowners with short sale experts for all 50 states. His seminars give the Industry an informative step by step solution for these difficult situations. As experience in foreclosure strategies this helps. His course helps identify each of the best options for the individual property owner and has developed a national website WholesaleProperties.com for marketing short sales for the Homeowner, Buyers, Realtors, Brokers and Agents.

Short Sales are the new "Tradition" for transactions today.

The President, Mark Cheeley was first licensed as a Real Estate licensee in the 1970's in Minnesota. He was actively in investments of multi-family units and managed for an investment group. In the 1990's, Mark Cheeley became a licensed Real Estate sales associate in the State of Florida and then Broker in 2002.

As an Author, Speaker and Real Estate Coach he developed a training course in 1993 of "Secret Win-Win Techniques and Foreclosure Strategies and How to Become a Foreclosure Consultant" teaching seminars to Realtors, Brokers and Agents in "Foreclosure Strategies".

Mark Cheeley is also the President of RiverBank Financial Corporation, a licensed mortgage broker and lender specializing in hard equity loans for Investors since 1987.

Mark Cheeley is the Founder and President of WholesaleProperties.com, a Real Estate Brokerage Business, in the State of Florida. WholesaleProperties.com was developed in 2000 to market bank owned properties to Investors on a national level for Buyers and Sellers.

In 2007, WholesaleProperties.com created an innovative website to market "On-Line Free Listing Service", the number one leading short sale and bank owned properties website. This was developed for buyers and sellers.

PREFACE

While a short sale is complex, our proven systems are a win-win solution for you. Due to our high success rate, our national foreclosure short sales team of experts are considered by some to be THE industry leaders.

The proven techniques of our course manual provide a step by step approach, or a two-process system. The first process is the Seller / Borrower package and the second process is the Coordinator / Processor / Lender / Investor package.

Once you have completed and understand our course, you will have the tools to accomplish win-win techniques of the short sale process. As a graduate of NFSSI, you will have access to support and free workshops by attending our local training centers in your area.

In our course manual, we present Seller / Borrower and Lender / Investor packages and the step by step procedures from the listing of the property to an actual offer for purchase of the short sale property. This begins the process of the Coordinator / Processor and Lender / Investor package.

Depending upon what state you are in you can go to the "State by State Method of Foreclosure" and find the citations of foreclosure methods if this is applicable to use for your listing and sale. The two significant packages will make the difference in the successful outcome.

To attain the best results from this course, first read the course materials from start to finish, then read the Sellers Package containing information 1 - 12 step by step methods. Simply familiarize yourself with the contents to obtain a listing from a Seller / Borrower. Our program will make more sense when you apply it to a short sale situation.

Once you obtain an offer from client (Buyer) or a Buyer's Agent, you can then proceed with our step by step Coordinator / Processor / Lender / Investor package the 1-12. Your reward will come from diligently pursuing and understanding the process of the Seller / Borrower package and the Coordinator / Processor / Lender / Investor package.

Our step by step method will make the process easier for you and assist you to reap the rewards of your efforts. Our National Foreclosure Short Sale Institute™ "Certified Expert" technical support team will be happy to answer all your questions for your ongoing support.

Table of Contents

Chapter 1: What is a Foreclosure? 9

Chapter 2: 20th Century Real Estate 14

    Market / The Short Pay 15

Chapter 3: 21st Century Real Estate / Short Sale 17

    3.1 FHA 22

    3.2 The HAFA Program 24

    3.3 HAMP 24

Chapter 4: Sub-Prime Crisis 31

    4.1 What Caused it? 32

    4.2 ARM/ Adjustable Rate Mortgages 32

Chapter 5: Types of Sub Prime Loan 34

    5.1 Products 35

Chapter 6: Security Devices 38

    6.1 Law Citations State by State Statutes 43

    6.2 Method of Foreclosure State by State 47

Chapter 7: Become a Certified Expert 49

Chapter 8: Borrower's Options 57

    8.1 Foreclosure 58

    8.2 Loan Modification 58

    8.3 Deed in Lieu 59

    8.4 Mortgage Reinstatement 59

    8.5 Forbearance 59

    8.6 Short Sale / Acceptable Hardships 60

Table of Contents

Chapter 9: Seller Package 65
9.1 Financial Statements 65
9.2 Federal Tax Returns 66
9.3 Pay Stubs / Proof of Income 66
9.4 Bank Accounts 67
9.5 Disclaimer 67
9.6 Acceptable Hardship Terms / HUD 67
9.7 Acceptable hardship terms / Short Sale 69
9.8 Authorization to Release Information 72
9.9 Exclusive Right of Sale Listing Agreement 72
9.10 Short Sale Addendum 73
9.11 Modification to Listing Agreement 73
9.12 Seller / Borrower Non-Performance Addendum 73
9.13 Arm's Length Transaction 74
9.14A Property Analysis Form and 9.14B Photo Log 74
9.15 Checklist 74

Chapter 10: Coordinator / Processing Services 77

Chapter 11: Jump Start your Wholesaling Business Now! 82
11.1 Submitting the Lender / Investor Package for Condition and Approval 117

Chapter 12: Problems to Avoid 122

Chapter 13: Non-Controllable Issues 124

Chapter 14: HUD - 1 Insert 126

Chapter 15: Frequently Asked Questions 129

Chapter 16: Title Frequently Asked Questions 136

Chapter 17: Web-Links 142

Chapter 18: Short Sale Definitions 147

Chapter 19: General Glossary Real Estate Terms 150

Chapter 1

What is a foreclosure?

CHAPTER 1 What is a foreclosure?

NOTES:

WHAT IS A FORECLOSURE?

---
*See the "Method of Foreclosure State by State"
Refer to Chapter 6*
---

1) State
2) Predominate Security Document (trust deed / mortgage)
3) Predominant Foreclosure Method (Judicial / strict foreclosure/ power of sale / entry & possession / mortgage)
4) Redemption Period (days / months)
5) Possession During Redemption (mortgagor / purchaser)
6) Deficiency Judgement (yes / no)

---
*See the "Law Citations State by State Statues"
Refer to Chapter 6*

Foreclosure is a legal process by which a Servicer / Lender / Investor, or other lien holder obtains a court ordered termination of a Borrower's equitable right of redemption. Usually a Servicer / Lender / Investor obtains a security interest from a borrower who mortgages or pledges an asset like a house to secure the loan. If the borrower defaults and the Servicer / Lender / Investor tries to repossess the property, courts can grant the borrower the equitable right of redemption if the borrower repays the debt. While this equitable right exists, the Servicer / Lender / Investor cannot be sure that it can successfully repossess the property, thus the Servicer / Lender / Investor seeks to foreclose the equitable right of redemption. Other lien holders can also foreclose the owner's right of redemption for other debts, such as for overdue taxes, unpaid contractor's bills, overdue homeowner association dues or assessments.

The foreclosure process as applied to mortgage loans is a Servicer / Lender / Investor or other secured creditor(s) selling or repossessing a parcel of real property (immovable property) after the owner has failed to comply with an agreement between the lender and

CHAPTER 1   What is a foreclosure?

borrower called a "mortgage" or "deed of trust". Commonly, the violation of the mortgage is a default in payment of a promissory note, secured by the lien on the property. When the process is complete, the lender can sell the property and keep the proceeds to pay off its mortgage and any legal costs, and it is typically said that Servicer / Lender / Investor has foreclosed its mortgage or lien. If the promissory note was made with a recourse clause and the sale does not bring enough to pay the existing balance of principle and fees, the Servicer / Lender / Investor can file a claim for a deficiency judgement.

FORECLOSURE DEFINITIONS

1) Default: Is when the Borrower(s) do not make their payments as a condition to the mortgage. The Servicer / Lender / Investor has the right to enforce legal proceedings. This can result in a public sale of the property covered by the lien with the proceeds of the sale used to pay / satisfy the lien holder's claim.

2) Lis Pendens: Is pending litigation. It is a filed document at the recorder's office in the county where the property is located to give public notice to all parties that the title to the affected property is in litigation. The Borrower has defaulted on the terms of their mortgage and may become subject to a judgment issued by the court. This public notice is considered constructive notice.

3) Equity of Redemption: Is the right of the Borrower during the foreclosure proceedings and prior to the notice of the public sale, to redeem their interest in the property by paying the full debt plus interest and legal cost.

CHAPTER 1 What is a foreclosure?

NOTES:

4) Notice of Sale: These are public filings, recordings, postings, notifications, and advertisements that are required by law. They are paid for by the Servicer / Lender / Investor. They will appear in many types of newspapers with small circulation. The charges and cost of the total legal process of the foreclosure will appear in the Summary Final Judgment of all money owed on the property. The Servicer / Lender / Investor receives the property back, as well as the fees and charges of the foreclosure process are then added to the cost of the summary final judgement.

5) Liens: In the legal proceedings of the foreclosure, there are superior and junior liens. The superior liens are priority to the junior liens. All the information concerning the title to a property is a matter of public record. Further, only the recorded information in the public records will enforce the priority of a lien over other claims.

6) Summary Final Judgment: Is a court document stating the final cost of the foreclosure proceeding. Including the principle balance, court cost, publication cost, attorney fees and any additional cost deemed by the court.

7) Deficiency Judgment: Is a court order requiring the Borrower to pay the difference of the balance remaining from the sale of the property against the balance owed to the Servicer / Lender / Investors.

Superior Liens: Take precedence over all junior liens

Federal Estate taxes

Property taxes

Special Assessments / Homeowners Associations (HOA)

CHAPTER 1 What is a foreclosure?

NOTES:

Junior Liens: Based on the date of recording

Federal Income Taxes

State Corporations Income tax

Mortgages

Vendors

Intangible tax

Judgements

Mechanic's Liens: This lien can date back and have a higher priority than other Junior Liens.

Please note: Throughout this manual we make references to Seller, Borrower, Lender, and Investor. In some cases, these may be multiple parties. i.e. Sellers, Borrowers, Lenders and Investors.

Chapter 2

20th Century Real Estate Market the Short Pay

20th CENTURY REAL ESTATE MARKET
THE SHORT PAY

The Summary of the Savings and Loan / Resolution Trust Corporation (RTC)

1) The institutions paid higher returns then they received.

2) The deregulation of the Savings and Loans led to the failure of the institutions.

3) The Tax Reform Act gave an incentive to the speculators.

4) The construction market overbuilt.

5) The unemployment levels are some of the highest since the great depression.

The Resolution Trust Corporation was formed to manage the assets and liquidations for over a thousand failed Savings and Loan Institutions.

The Resolution Trust Corporation (known as RTC) was created in 1989 to assume the management of insolvent Savings and Loan Associations in order to sell their assets in the form of loans under guidelines set up by the Financial Institutions Reform / Recovery and Enforcement Act. This was also known as the (F.I.R.R.E.A.). The objective was to protect depositors hard earned money deposited to these institutions.

There were methods used by RTC when it took over to dispose of assets. The first was Conservatorship in which RTC arranged the sale of the assets and deposits while that institution remained open and continued to do business. Once all the assets were sold the institutions were closed.

The second method was Receivership. When the institution closed the RTC it became the receiver of the remaining assets which had not been liquidated. All remaining real estate assets were marketed through brokers who were supervised by the RTC.

The real estate assets under the control of RTC were independently appraised and then placed on the market to potential buyers. Due to the tremendous number of properties held by the RTC, private firms obtained rights to them through a competitive bidding process. The RTC listing brokers were the contact people when purchasing RTC property.

This was done through a process similar to the conventional method whereas buyer / investor(s) were dealing directly with the RTC broker for showing the property, executing a contract and other documents.

A "Portfolio Sale" was another means when purchasing RTC property. This was accomplished through a sealed bid auction method. Lastly, is the auction method. This seemed to be the wave of the 90»s and was a great way to get bargain prices. RTC auction information was obtained from the nearest RTC sales center.

RTC sales centers were located throughout the country for information, guidance and assistance in purchasing or obtaining real estate property.

Time heals all wounds...

---

*The historical cycle returns in the
21st century the Short Sale.*

Chapter 3

21st Century Real Estate
The Short Sale

21st CENTURY REAL ESTATE MARKET
THE SHORT SALE

The Summary of the Sub-Prime Mortgage Crisis

The United States sub-prime mortgage crisis has led to plunging property prices, a slowdown in the United States economy, and billions of dollars in losses by Banks, Lenders, and Investors.

It stems from a fundamental change in the way mortgages are funded.

Traditionally, banks have financed their mortgages lending through the deposits they received from depositors.

This has limited the amount of mortgage lending they could do.

In recent years, banks have moved to a new model where they sell the mortgages to the secondary mortgage market.

This has made it much easier to fund additional borrowing, but it has also led to abuse, as banks no longer have the incentive to carefully check the mortgages, they issue.

The Rise of the Mortgage Bond Market

In the past five years, the private sector has dramatically expanded its role in the mortgage bond market, which had previously been dominated by government sponsored agencies like Freddie Mac.

The specialization in these new types of mortgages, lead to sub-prime lending to borrowers with poor credit histories and weak documentation of income. Previously these borrowers were shunned by the "prime" lenders like Freddie Mac.

The Crisis Is Nationwide

Sub-Prime lending spread from inner-city areas throughout America by 2005. By then, one in five mortgages were sub-prime.

Sub-Prime mortgages also had a much higher rate of default and repossession than conventional mortgages because they were adjustable rate mortgages (ARMs).

Consequently, a wave of repossessions is sweeping America as many of these mortgages reset to higher rates. Making the monthly payment unaffordable for the borrower.

It is likely that as many as two million families will default on their mortgage payments and be evicted from their homes as their cases make their way through the courts.

The wave of repossessions is having a dramatic effect on housing prices, reversing the housing boom of the last few years and causing the first national decline in house prices since the Great Depression.

There is also an overstock of four million unsold new homes that are depressing prices. Builders have also been forced to lower prices to liquidate their unsold properties.

Housing and the Economy

The Sub-Prime Crisis, and resulting collapse in the Real Estate market, has had a major negative impact on the US economy. This has resulted in the devastation of the building industry and the loss of millions of jobs.

The building industry makes up 15% of the United States housing economy. The slow down effects other industries such as durable goods, appliances, home furniture, and home repair. Many smaller builders went bankrupt along with some large builders went completely out of business due to the huge losses.

Historical Records of Unemployment

In the year 2000, The United States experienced a 10% National rate of unemployment, the highest since the 1980's. (see The Misery Index: http://www.miseryindex.us/urbmonth.asp)

The United State consumers have spent beyond their current income by borrowing on their home equity.

Credit Crunch

Banks and Lenders are rejecting more people who are applying for credit cards, also reducing the lines of credit card limits.

They are insisting on bigger deposits on house purchases and looking more closely at applications for loans.

As the properties are underwater there is no equity, they owe more on the mortgage then the market value.

Bond Market Collapse

The collapse of the bond market effected not only the United States but the world.

Bond holders and pension funds holders suffered huge losses in the sub-prime mortgage bonds.

As the rating agency rated the original value of the asset higher than it was. This revealed that financial institutions were taking billions of dollars in losses.

Bank Losses

The banking industry took advantage of the changing finance laws in the mortgage industry, facing huge losses as the result.

As the bank took off balance instruments called Structured Investment Vehicles (SIVS), this concealed the exposure of the sub-prime mortgage in the banking industry.

As a result, the banks were liable for their losses and forced to cover any bad instrument as they occurred.

The historical cycle returns to the 21st century.

As history repeats itself, "TIME HEALS ALL WOUNDS"

An overview of the following facts:

1) Unemployment rates are very high.

2) The construction market is over-built.

3) 50% of home ownership is underwater due to the rapid deprecation of property value.

4) Historically there has never been so many multiple hardships facing the homeowner.

5) The Federal Deposit Insurance Corporation (FDIC) obtained ownership of hundreds of financial institutions and transferred ownership to highly successful solvent financial institutions.

The Federal Deposit Insurance Corporation (FDIC) went into a partnership with these financial institutions.

As this sub-prime mortgage crisis is resulting in record numbers of failed financial institutions, it created a market collapse.

3.1 FHA Is Now the Most Popular program

The Federal Housing Association (FHA) is part of HUD and insures the loan, so your lender can offer you a better deal. FHA loans have been helping people become homeowners since 1934.

Some of the advantages are:
- Low down payments
- Low closing costs
- Easy credit qualifying

GNMA, FNMA, and FHLMC are the three largest buyers of residential mortgage loans on the secondary mortgage market, a place where trillions of dollars in existing mortgage loans are traded.

GNMA Government National Mortgage Association (Ginnie Mae)
- Created in 1934 to help recover from the depression
- Funding comes from agency bonds
- Will purchase or securitize government backed loans such as FHA, VA, USDA

FNMA Federal National Mortgage Association (Fannie Mae)
- Created in 1934 by Congress
- Funding comes from agency bonds
- Will purchase or securitize conventional loans (non-government backed loans) and FHA, VA loans
- Has and automated underwriting system called Desktop Underwriter

FHLMC Federal Home Loan Mortgage Corporation (Freddie Mac)
- Authorized in 1968 by Congress
- Funding comes from agency bonds
- Will purchase or securitize conventional loans
- Has and automated underwriting system called Loan Prospector

The Federal Housing Financial Agency sets the criteria for what loans Fannie Mae and Freddie Mac can buy. Consult your Federal Loan Originator for the guidelines in your market.

National Servicing Center
www.hud.gov/offices/hsg/sfh/nsc/nschome.cfm

Email: hsg-lossmit@hud.gov
1-888-297-8685

Frequently Asked Questions:
http://www.hud.gov/offices/hsg/sfh/sfh/nsc/lmmltrs.cfm

3.2 THE HAFA PROGRAM

Introduction

HAFA is a new Government program that provides additional options to avoid costly foreclosures and offers incentives to borrowers, servicers and investors who utilize a short sale or deed-in-lieu (DIL) to avoid foreclosures.

Home Affordable Modification Program (HAMP)

If your Lender grants you a modification after many months of deliberating, they will take the amount you are behind and add it to the balance (This puts you further behind since you probably ALREADY owe more on the house then it is worth). If you are lucky, they will drop your interest rates a couple of points. However, due to the amount they put back on to your balance, your saving will not be very significant.

A study from the Mortgage Banker Association of modified loans showed that close to 90% of the homeowner were in foreclosure again within two years.

3.3 HAMP - The second lien modification program is for homeowners who are struggling with payments in part because of a second lien on their home. For those who are eligible the program offers a way to lower payments on their second mortgage. 2MP is a complementary program to the Home Affordable Modification Program (HAMP), so it is meant for those who have already modified their first mortgage through HAMP.

The Servicer / Lender / Investor consider (HAMP) eligible borrowers for (HAFA) within 30 days of the date of the borrower:

- Does not qualify for trial period plan.
- Does not successfully complete trial period plan
- Is delinquent on HAMP modification by missing at least two consecutive payments.

Requests a short sale or Deed-in-Lieu

Deed in Lieu of Foreclosure

The bank still may have the right to pursue for a deficiency judgment and if you have a second mortgage, they will most likely not agree unless you sign a promissory note for the balance. You still must pay the second mortgage!

This (HAFA) program allows the borrower not to have a deficiency judgment. (does not apply in California, Minnesota, Mississippi, Montana, North Dakota and West Virginia)

The Servicer / Lender / Investor must proactively notify the

Servicer / Lender / Investor allows borrower(s) 14 calendar days to contact them with interest in these options. After this timeline, Servicer / Lender / Investor has no further obligation to extent the HAFA offer.

SHORT SALE

A short sale is when a Servicer / Lender / Investor will take less then what is owed on the mortgage of the borrower.

A Short Sale is Truly the Homeowners Best Options!

The Servicer / Lender / Investor must proactively notify the borrower in writing the availability of a short sale.

Servicer / Lender / Investor allows borrower(s) 14 calendar days to contact them with interest in these options. After this timeline, Servicer / Lender / Investor has no further obligation to extend the HAFA offer.

INCENTIVES - (FOR ALL PARTIES)

BORROWER

1. Entitled to a payment of $3,000 to assist with relocation expenses.
2. The Lender / Investor waves all rights to seek a deficiency judgment and may not require the borrower to sign a promissory note for the deficiency.
3. Borrower is not required to bring money for closing.

SERVICER

1. $1,500 will be paid to cover administrative and processing costs.

LENDER / INVESTOR

1. $2,000 to Investors for subordinate lien holder payoff.
For every three dollars spent to release liens (up to $6,000) buyer or investor is reimbursed one dollar (up to $2,000).

Conditions:

Home Affordable Foreclosure Alternatives (HAFA) Program effective dates are from April 5, 2010 to December 31, 2012.

Listing must be done by a licensed Real Estate Professional. The servicer cannot reduce the reduction of the commission agreed upon by the seller (not to exceed 6% of the contract sales price).

1) Property is borrower's primary residence and may not be vacant more than 90 days.
2) Loan is a first lien and originated on or before January 1, 2009.
3) Loan is delinquent or default is reasonably foreseeable
4) Current unpaid balance is or less than $729,750
5) Total monthly mortgage payment exceeds 31% of borrowers monthly gross income.

Processing / Timeline / Exhibits

Servicer / Lender / Investor (The following below items to be completed by the servicer.)

A) Short Sale Agreement (HAFA Program)

Timeline: Within 30 days the borrower must request a short sale agreement.

Process: The following 1-13 are completed by the servicer:

1. List Price or Acceptable Sale Proceeds
2. Listing Agreement
2a. Cancellation Clause
2b. Listing Agreement Contingency Clause
3. Property Maintenance and Expenses
4. Partial Mortgage Payments
5. Allowable Cost that may be deducted Gross from Sales Proceeds
5a. Closing Costs
5b. Subordinate Liens
5c. Real Estate Commissions
5d. Borrower Relocation Assistance
6. Sales Contract
7. Parties to the Sale
8. Closing
9. Foreclosure Sale Suspension
10. Satisfaction and Release of Liability
11. Mortgage Insurer or Guarantor Approval
12. Termination of this Agreement
13. Settlement of Debt

Exhibit Forms:

A-1) Request for Short Sale (HAFA)

Timeline: N/A
Process: A - I

A. Terms
B. Changes
C. Subordinate Liens
D. HUD - 1
E. Bankruptcy
F. Tax Consequences
G. Credit Bureau Reporting
H. Payment Instructions
I. Closing Instructions

Exhibit Forms:
B) Alternative Request for Approval of Short Sale (HAFA)

Timeline: 14 Calendar days from date of the request
Process: 1 - 9

1. Allowable Costs that May be Deducted from Gross Sale Price
1a. Closing Cost
1b. Subordinate Liens
1c. Real Estate Commissions
1d. Borrower Relocation Assistance
2. Property Maintenance and Expense
3. Particle Mortgage Payments
4. Parties to the Sale
5. Foreclosure Sale Suspension
6. Satisfaction and Release of Liability
7. Mortgage Insurer or Guarantor Approval
8. Termination of This Request
8a. You fail to provide all the required documents listed above
8b. Your financial situation improves significantly, you qualify for a modification, you bring the account current or you pay off the mortgage in full.
8c. You or your broker fails to act in good faith in closing

on the sale of the property or otherwise fails to abide by the terms of this request.
8d. A significant change occurs to the property conditions or value.
8e. There is evidence of fraud or misrepresentation.
8f. You file for bankruptcy and the Bankruptcy Court declines to approve the A Request.

8g. Litigation is initiated or threatened that could affect title to the property or interfere with a valid conveyance.
8h. You do not make the payments required under this Request.
9. Settlement of Debt.

C) DIL (Deed-in-Lieu) Agreement (HAFA)

Timeline: Within 14 calendar days, the Borrower must request a DIL Agreement.
Process: 1-10

1. Property Maintenance and Expense
2. Partial Mortgage Payments
3. Borrower Relocation Assistance
4. Foreclosure Sale Suspension
5. Satisfaction and Release of Liability
6. Mortgage Insured or Guarantor Approval
7. Termination of This Agreement
7a. Your financial situation improves significantly, you qualify for loan modification, you bring the account current or you pay off the mortgage in full.
7b. You fail to act in good faith with the Agreement
7c. A significant change occurs to the property condition or value
7d. There is evidence of fraud or misrepresentation.
7e. You file for bankruptcy and the Bankruptcy Court declines to approve the agreement
7f. Litigation is initiated or threatened that could affect title to the property or interfere with the valid conveyance

7g. You do not make the payments required under this Agreement.
8. Settlement of a Debt
9. Possible Incomes Tax Considerations
10. Credit Bureau Reporting

HAFA LINKS

HAFA Link
https://www.hmpadmin.com/portal/programs/foreclosurealternatives.jsp

HAMP Link
http://www.makinghomeaffordable.com/contact_servicer.html

HAMP Handbook
https://www.hmpadmin.com/portal/programs/docs/hamp_servicer/mhahandbook_30.pdf

Freddie Mack Link
http://www.freddiemac.com/avoidforeclosure/

Chapter 4

Sub-Prime Crisis: What Caused It?

SUB-PRIME CRISIS

4.1 WHAT CAUSED IT?

Understanding the Sub-Prime Loans.

Lenders offered mortgage products to customers that were ultimately not qualified to obtain.

Either through terms the customer didn't understand or because of adjusting interest rates combined with negative amortization and hefty prepayment penalties.

4.2 ARM / Adjustable rate mortgages were calculated on variable interest rates.

1) Index commonly used as the bases for the adjustable rate mortgages (ARMS) called London Inter Bank Lending Rate (LIBOR) or Monthly Treasury Average (MTA).

The Index, also called the Prime Lending Rate, is not a relatively stable index. It fluctuates.

2) Margin is set by the financial Institution/Lender. It is an amount that the Lender adds to an index to calculate and determine the interest rate on an adjustable rate mortgage.

Depending upon the loan product written, it could actually increase over time.

3) The borrower's rate is the index plus the margin.

CHAPTER 4 Sub-Prime Crisis - What Caused It?

THIS COMBINATION WAS WRITTEN FOR FINANCIAL FAILURE.

The borrowers whose monthly mortgage payments did not include a portion for taxes and insurance.

A lot of borrowers who received subprime mortgages had credit scores below 600.

The products available to the Borrower were written mostly based on a temporary teaser rates or introductory rate.

This allowed Borrowers to pick a price and not necessarily understand the kind of loan package that was offered to them. These products in time double, tripled, and quadrupled the Borrowers payments. It was one of the factors of this crisis.

> *"This caused financial suicide for many homeowners."*

There were no options to stop the bleeding.

Homeowners unable to make their mortgage payments were left with very few options.

The Mortgage Loan Originator on these products took advantage of the Borrower as they gave the Borrower the product that fit the Originators highest income.

So, the factor was the worst exotic products for the Borrower and was the highest Yield Spread Premium (YSP), the loan originator. This spread was as much as two to three times tripling the mortgage loan originators income.

> *This is the reason so many Borrowers were given Sub-Prime loans.*

Chapter 5

Types of Sub-Prime Loan Products

CHAPTER 5 Types of Sub-Prime Loan Products

5.1 TYPES OF SUB-PRIME LOAN PRODUCTS

The borrowers provided information to the Lenders to obtain the mortgages product, it was not always accurate and truthful.

A possible mortgage fraud could have been committed to purchase their home. By inflated income, assets and provided documentation it could become a criminal offense to the homeowner.

1) **Interest Only:** Interest was paid on the original amount of the mortgage for a period that had an expired yearly term. There was no monthly payment applied to the principle / original amount.

2) **100%:** The Borrower paid a premium interest rate and insurance premium called Private Mortgage Insurance (PMI). This gave the opportunity to the Borrower for no down payment.

3) **125%:** This was opportunity for the Borrower to walk away at closing with cash. This was commonly used in accelerating property values.

4) **80/20:** The Lender financed 80% of the purchase price to make a first mortgage and an additional or same Lender then financed 20% of the purchase price on a second mortgage. The lenders risk on the second mortgage is higher than the first with these two monthly mortgage payments it made it a struggle for the homeowner. Often the second mortgage is higher due to Private Mortgage Insurance (PMI) premium.

5) **40/50 Year Term:** This allowed the Borrower to extend the term of the years. This was a lower monthly payment, this resulted in a higher cost of the home over time.

CHAPTER 5 Types of Sub Prime Loan Products

6) Stated Income / Verified Assets (SIVA): This allowed the Borrower to *state* their income without any salary documentation, verification of employment only. The asset conditions were the requirements by the Lender of proof of funds. A credit score was a factor.

7) Stated Income / Stated Assets (SISA): This allowed the Borrower to *state* their income without any salary documentation, verification of employment only. The asset and income conditions were just stated, no back up documents were required. A credit score was a factor.

8) No Income / No Assets (NINA): A credit score was a large factor, it stood on the credit score. The condition for this was a lower loan to value, with a required large down payment. There was no documentation required for income or assets.

9) No Doc: A required credit score, contact information, signature and a *pulse*.

10) The NINJA: Conditions were NO Income, NO Job, or NO Assets.

11) LIAR Loans: All requirements were *stated* and not verified.

12) Adjustable Rate Mortgages (ARM): ARM - The index and the margin are combined. Both the index and the mortgage rates fluctuated.

2/28: The interest rate increased for a period of term with a cap rate. In this case a 2 year fixed interest rate followed by adjustable every year for 28 years thereafter.

3/27: The interest rate increased for a period of term with a cap rate.

Options: The Borrower had an option to choose payment amounts and term.

Neg Am: A negative am is deferred interest and/or deferred principle in which the balance of the loan goes up and not down with each payment.

Chapter 6

Security Devices

CHAPTER 6 Security Devices

SECURITY DEVICE - POWER OF SALE

A clause commonly inserted in a Mortgage and Deed of Trust that grants the creditor or Trustee the right and authority, upon default in the payment of the debt, to advertise and sell the property at public auction, without resorting to a Court for authorization to do so.

Once the creditor is paid out of the net proceeds, the property is transferred by deed to the purchaser, and the surplus, if any, is returned to the debtor. The debtor is thereby completely divested of his or her interest in the property and has no subsequent right of redemption - recovery of property by paying the mortgage debt in full.

West Publishing Company
The American Guide to American Law
Volume 8, Page 250

SECURITY DEVICE - DEED OF TRUST - TRUST DEED

There are states (i.e. California) that use Trust Deeds (Deeds of Trust) instead of the common Mortgage. Both documents have similarities. They promise the borrowers (trustors) property as security for the loan. The difference in this type of format is that the lender (beneficiary) doesn't hold the mortgage. A third party known as a Trustee holds the lien against the property. More often than not, the Trustee is a Title Company. A Trust Deed allows the trustee to auction property without court involvement. This is permitted through a special item in the deed known as a power-of-sale clause. This feature attracts lenders. They much prefer trust deeds to mortgages based mainly on the aforementioned clause.

There are three parties to a Deed of Trust or Trust Deed:

1) The Beneficiary (lender)
2) The Trustor (borrower)
3) The Trustee (Stakeholder)

The Trustee is a third party who is independent of the lender or the borrower. This can be a Title Company, an Escrow Company, or a Trust Company which is specifically set up to act as the third party. The lender makes the loan and the borrower signs the deed. This is then called a "Trust Deed" to the Trustee. If or when the borrower fails to make the payments, the deed enables the trustee to sell the property and pay the lender.

The difference between a "Mortgage" and a "Trust Deed" is that property in default on a "Mortgage" must go through court action to sell the property and regain the amount in default, whereas, in a Trust Deed the Trustee is empowered to sell the property when it goes into default.

SECURITY DEVICE - MORTGAGE

The Mortgage document provide the necessary security the lender requires so that the terms set forth in the contract are properly honored. The Mortgage, in effect, guarantees the lender that his money will be repaid to him. The written instrument known as a Mortgage pledges a particular property to guarantee that the money will be repaid. The borrower gives a voluntary lien (claim) to the lender. The borrower is stating clearly through the lien that if he doesn't pay the money owed, the lender has the right to the property which can be sold so that he can recuperate his money.

Many of our states (i.e. Florida) are lien theory states. This means that although the borrower holds the title to a certain property, the lender has the right to foreclose through a court procedure to gain title of the property if the terms of the agreement are not met.

When there is a first and second mortgage on a property, commonly the second mortgage holder forces the sale. Generally, if payments have not been made on the second mortgage, the first mortgage is also in default and the first mortgage holder would be the first party to receive payment from a forced sale. In order for the second mortgage holder to recover his interest on this deed, he should include the amount of indebtedness on the first mortgage and bring the first mortgage holder cur- rent (preventing them from foreclosing). This procedure ensures the second mortgage holder the total amount claimed in his foreclosure action. If he fails to do this, he must be satisfied with payment of any overage that might be available after the first mortgage holder is paid from a forced sale.

CHAPTER 6 Security Devices

NOTES:

FORECLOSURE LAW CITATIONS

You will find a comprehensive list of the foreclosure law citations from each of our fifty states called Law Citations State by State in this manual.

You need to take the citation information for your particular state from the list to a law library, the librarian can help you find the volume you need to study and understand. You can also do internet searches. Learn as much as you can about your state's laws regarding foreclosure. It is wise to make copies of the material so that you can always have it at hand for reference and for further study.

Laws are complex. You might need help to interpret them. Contact an attorney who specializes and is really knowledgeable in your state's real estate law. Call the American Bar Association 1-800-285-2221 and this referral service will give you information about attorneys who can help you.

You must understand that you are not providing legal assistance. You are a foreclosure consultant. Your client must understand this also. Never allow your client to believe that you are giving legal advice covering foreclosure proceedings.

Your role as a foreclosure consultant is to give assistance to your clients, not legal services. The system we have developed for you will work.

NOTE: You must check the method of foreclosure state by state to decide that the security device is either a Mortgage, Trust Deed / Deed of Trust. (SEE Appendix)

CHAPTER 6 Security Devices

NOTES:

6.1 LAW CITATIONS STATE BY STATE

Alabama	Code of Alabama, Vol. 6, Title 6, Sections 6-5-240 et seq.; Vol. 19 Title 35 Sections 35-10-1 et seq.
Alaska	Alaska Statues, Vol. 2, Title 9, Sections 09.45.170 et seq.; Title 34, Sections 34.20.070 et seq.
Arizona	Revised Statutes, Annotated, Vol. 4A, Title 12, Sections 12-1281 et seq.; Vol. 11, Title 33, Sections 33-721 et seq.; 33-807
Arkansas	Arkansas Statutes Annotated, Vol. 5, Sections 51-1105 et seq.; Vol. 7B, Sections 84-1201
California	California Civil Code Sections 2920 et seq., 2945 et seq., 1695 et seq.
Colorado	Colorado Revised Statutes 1973, Vol. 16, Title 38, Sections 38-37-101 et seq., 38-39-101 et seq.
Connecticut	Connecticut General Statutes Annotated, Vol. 22A, Sections 49-14, 49-17 et seq.,
Delaware	Delaware Code Annotated, Vol. 6, Sections 10-4716; 10-4961 et seq., 10-5061 et seq.
Florida	Florida Statutes Annotated, Vol. 2, Sections 45.031; Vol. 20, section 702.01
Georgia	Georgia Code Annotated, Book 20, Sections 67-115 et seq. 67-201, 67-401, 67-701, 67-1503, et seq.
Hawaii	Hawaii Revised Statutes, Vol. 71, Sections 677-1 et seq.
Idaho	Idaho Code, Vol. 2, Sections 5-226 et seq., 6-101, 11-301 et seq., 11-401
Illinois	Illinois Code of Civil Procedure, Sections 12-122 et seq., 15-101 et seq.
Indiana	Burns» Indiana Statutes Annotated, Sections 32-8-16-1, 31-8-17-1, 34-1-19-4 et seq., 34-2-29-3

CHAPTER 6 Security Devices

NOTES:

Iowa	Iowa Code Annotated, Vol. 50, Sections 628.2 et seq., 654.1
Kansas	Kansas Statutes Annotated, Vol. 4, Sections 58-2253 et seq., 58-2314 et seq.; Vol. 4A, Sections 60-2410 et seq.
Kentucky	Baldwin's Kentucky revised Statutes, Vol. 7, Sections 426.200 et seq.
Louisiana	Louisiana Revised Statutes, Vol. 6, Article 2343; Vol. 10, Article 2568 Code of Civil Procedure; Vol. 7 4106, 4341 et seq., Vol. 8 4942 et seq.
Maine	Maine revised Statutes Annotated, Vol. 7, Sections 14-2151, 14-2202 et seq., 14-2251 et seq., Vol. 8, Sections 14-6201 et seq.
Maryland	Annotated Code of Maryland, Vol. 9C, Rule W70 et seq., BR6
Massachusetts	Annotated Laws of Massachusetts, Chapter 244, Section 244-1 et seq., 244-17A, 244-35
Michigan	Michigan Statutes Annotated, Vol. 22, Sections 27A.3140, 27A.3201 et seq.
Minnesota	Minnesota Statutes Annotated, Vol. 37, Sections 580.02 et seq., 581.10, 582.14 et seq.
Mississippi	Mississippi Code 1972 Annotated, Vol. 5, Section 15-1-19 et seq., Vol. 19, Section 89-1-53 et seq.
Missouri	Vernon's Annotated Missouri Statutes, Vol. 23, Sections 443.290 et seq.
Montana	Montana Code Annotated 1981, Vol. 3, Sections 25-13-801 et seq.
Nebraska	Revised Statutes of Nebraska, Vol. 2, Sections 25-1530; 25-2137 et seq.
Nevada	Nevada Revised Statutes, Vol. 2, Sections 21.130 et seq.; Vol. 3, Section 40.430; Vol. 5, Sections 106.025, 107.080 et seq.

CHAPTER 6 Security Devices

NOTES:

New Hampshire	New Hampshire Revised Statutes Annotated, Vol. 4A, Sections 479.19 et seq.; Vol. 5, Section 529.26
New Jersey	New Jersey Statutes Annotated
New Mexico	New Mexico Statutes 1978 Annotated, Vol. 6, Sections 39-5-1, 39-5-19 et seq.; Vol. 7, Sections 48-3-14, 48-7-7
New York	McKinney's Consolidated Laws of New York Annotated; Book 49 1/2, Sections 1352, 1401 et seq.
N. Carolina	General Statutes of North Carolina, Vol. 1, Sections 1-47; Vol. 2A, Sections 45-21.1 et seq.
N. Dakota	North Dakota Century Code Annotated, Vol. 5A, Sections 28-24-01 et seq.; Vol. 6, Section 32-19-1, 32-19-18, Vol. 7, Sections 35-22-01 et seq.
Ohio	Page's Ohio revised Code Annotated, Title 23, Section 2323
Oklahoma	Oklahoma Statutes Annotated, Section 12-686, 12-764, 46-31 et seq., 46-301
Oregon	Oregon Revised Statutes, Vol. 1, Sections 86-010, 86-710 et seq., 88-040 et seq.
Pennsylvania	Purdon's Pennsylvania Statutes Annotated, Title 72, Sections 403 et seq.,
Rhode Island	General Laws of Rhode Island, Vol. 6, Sections 34-23-1 et seq., 34-26-1, 34-27-1 et seq.
S. Carolina	Code of Laws of South Carolina 1976, Vol. 7, Sections 15-39-640 et seq., Vol. 10, Sections 29-3-10, 29-3-630 et seq.
S. Dakota	South Dakota Codified Laws 1967, Vol. 6, Section 15-19-23; Vol. 7, Sections 21-52-2 et seq.
Tennessee	Tennessee Code Annotated, Vol. 4, Sections 16-16-111, 21-1-803, 35-501 et seq., 66-8-101

CHAPTER 6 Security Devices

NOTES:

Texas	Vernon's Civil Statutes of the State of Texas Annotated, Vol. 12, Title 56, Articles 3810, 3819 et seq.; 1982 Texas Rules of Court, Rule #309
Utah	Utah Code Annotated 1953 (1977), Vol. 9A, Sections 78-37-1, 78-40-8; Vol. 9B, Rules of Civil Procedure 80.1 (e) (h)
Virginia	Code of Virginia, Vol. 8, Sections 55-59 et seq.
Washington	Revised Code of Washington annotated, Title 6, Sections 6.24.010 et seq.; Title 61, Section 61.12.060
W. Virginia	West Virginia Code, Vol. 11, Sections 38-1-1A et seq.; Vol. 16, Sections 59-3-1 et seq.
Wisconsin	West's Wisconsin Statutes Annotated, Section 815.31, 846.51 et seq.
Wyoming	Wyoming Statutes Annotated, Vol. 2, Sections 1-18-101 et seq.; Vol. 7, Sections 34-4-102 et seq.

6.2 METHOD OF FORECLOSURE (STATE BY STATE)

STATE	PREDOMINANT SECURITY DOCUMENT	PREDOMINANT FORECLOSURE METHOD	REDEMPTION PERIOD	POSSESSION DURING REDEMPTION	DEFICIENCY JUDGEMENT
Alabama	Mortgage	Power of Sale	12 mos.	Purchaser	Yes
Alaska	Trust Deed	Power of Sale	None		Yes
Arizona	Trust Deed	Power of Sale	None		Yes
Arkansas	Mortgage	Power of Sale	12 mos.		Yes
California	Trust Deed	Power of Sale	None		No
Colorado	Trust Deed	Power of Sale	75 days	Mortgagor	Yes
Connecticut	Mortgage	Power of Sale	None		Yes
Delaware	Mortgage	Judicial	None		Yes
D.C.	Trust Deed	Power of Sale	None		Yes
Florida	Mortgage	Judicial	10 days		Yes
Georgia	Security Deed	Power of Sale	None		Yes
Hawaii	Trust Deed	Power of Sale	None		Yes
Idaho	Trust Deed	Power of Sale	None		Yes
Illinois	Mortgage	Judicial	12 mos.	Mortgagor	Yes
Indiana	Mortgage	Judicial	3 mos.	Mortgagor	Yes
Iowa	Mortgage	Judicial	6 mos.	Mortgagor	Yes
Kansas	Mortgage	Judicial	12 mos.	Mortgagor	Yes
Kentucky	Mortgage	Judicial	None		Yes
Louisiana	Mortgage	Judicial	None		Yes
Maine	Mortgage	Entry & Possession	12 mos.	Mortgagor	Yes
Maryland	Trust Deed	Power of Sale	None		Yes
Massachusetts	Mortgage	Power of Sale	None		Yes
Michigan	Mortgage	Power of Sale	6 mos.		Yes
Minnesota	Mortgage	Power of Sale	6 mos.	Mortgagor	No
Mississippi	Trust Deed	Power of Sale	None		No

METHOD OF FORECLOSURE (STATE BY STATE)

STATE	PREDOMINANT SECURITY DOCUMENT	PREDOMINANT FORECLOSURE METHOD	REDEMPTION PERIOD	POSSESSION DURING REDEMPTION	DEFICIENCY JUDGEMENT
Missouri	Trust Deed	Power of Sale	12 mos.	Mortgagor	YES
Montana	Mortgage	Judicial	12 mos.	Mortgagor	NO
Nebraska	Mortgage	Judicial	None		YES
Nevada	Mortgage	Power of Sale	None		YES
New Hampshire	Mortgage	Power of Sale	None		YES
New Jersey	Mortgage	Judicial	10 days		YES
New Mexico	Mortgage	Judicial	1 mo.	Purchaser	YES
New York	Mortgage	Judicial	None		YES
N. Carolina	Trust Deed	Power of Sale	None		YES
N. Dakota	Mortgage	Judicial	12 mos.	Mortgagor	NO
Ohio	Mortgage	Judicial	None		YES
Oklahoma	Mortgage	Judicial	None		YES
Oregon	Trust Deed	Power of Sale	None		YES
Pennsylvania	Mortgage	Judicial	None		YES
Rhode Island	Mortgage	Power of Sale	None		YES
S. Carolina	Mortgage	Judicial	None		YES
S. Dakota	Mortgage	Power of Sale	12 mos.	Mortgagor	YES
Tennessee	Trust Deed	Power of Sale	None		YES
Texas	Trust Deed	Power of Sale	None		YES
Utah	Mortgage	Judicial	6 mos.	Mortgagor	YES
Vermont	Mortgage	Strict Foreclosure	6 mos.	Mortgagor	YES
Virginia	Mortgage	Power of Sale	None		YES
Washington	Mortgage	Judicial	12 mos.	Mortgagor	YES
W. Virginia	Trust Deed	Power of Sale	None		NO
Wisconsin	Mortgage	Power of Sale	None		YES
Wyoming	Mortgage	Power of Sale	6 mos.	Mortgagor	YES

Chapter 7

Become a Certified Expert

BECOME A CERTIFIED EXPERT

Realtor, Broker and Agents

Are you looking to increase your pipeline of business?

---
*Soaring to new levels of success
in the new "Tradition" of short sales.*

While a short sale is complex, our proven systems are a Win - Win solution for your efforts.

Due to our high success rate, our national foreclosure short sales team experts are the industry leaders.

Brand yourself as a NFSSI "Certified Expert"SM.

Why become a Certified Expert?

Only one percent of the 1.1 million Realtors are doing short sales according to a survey from the National Association of Realtors.

According to a survey by the National Association of Realtors, almost 40% to 50% of all existing homes sold in the recent months were either short sales or foreclosures. Of all the active listings on Multiple Listing Service 60% are short sales. Short sales are exploding at extreme levels and the media coverage is daily. As this is a win-win solution for your seller as the process is fee free.

Below are the listing short sales from the Multiple Listing Service:

2008   21% of Sales
2009   43% of Sales
2010   65% of Sales

The Census Bureau says: "There are two million vacant homes for sale, double the historic level."

90% of the homes currently are in foreclosure and have no equity or Underwater.

Ten million homes (which represent 13% of the delinquent mortgages) are going to fall behind in the fourth quarter of 2010 and the beginning of 2011.

The Mortgage Bankers Association says that the Lender / Investor will save 15% in losses by doing a short sale verses a foreclosure. The average cost to the Lender / Investor on a foreclosure is $44,000 as the short sale is less at $21,000. This is why the Lender / Investor is willing to take the short sale.

Why Should Your Seller / Borrower Do A Short Sale?

Options:

Foreclosure

If Seller / Borrower does nothing... The Lender will or has already filed foreclosure action against them, and eventually will attempt to sell their home at a sheriff sale, they will not receive anywhere close to what they owe on the property. The lender has the option to sue them and obtained a deficiency judgement for the difference between the total amount that was owed (including fees) and the amount they were able to sell it for. The borrower will have a foreclosure on their credit report for 10 years or more and will not be able to buy another home with conventional financing for MANY, MANY years.

Going through the foreclosure can knock 200 points off a FICO score, five times as much as the penalty for a short sale.

As the reporting of a short sale on their credit report drops 40 points average.

Loan Modification

If their Lender grants them a modification after many months of deliberating, they will take the amount they are behind and add it to the balance (This puts them further behind since they probably ALREADY owe more on the house then it is worth). If they are lucky, the Lender will drop the interest rates a couple of points. However, due to the amount they put back on to the balance, the savings will not be very significant. A study from the mortgage association of modified loans showed that close to 90% of the homeowners were in foreclosure again within two years.

Deed in Lieu of Foreclosure

The bank still may have the right to pursue a deficiency judgement. If they have a second mortgage, they will most likely not agree unless the Seller / Borrower signs a promissory note for the balance. They still must pay the second mortgage!!! This will also have a very negative impact on their credit rating!

(Does not apply in California, Minnesota, Mississippi, Montana, North Dakota and West Virginia)

Short Sale

Good News for Your Seller / Borrower

The "American Dream" can come back!

The Seller / Borrower has these options once your successful short sale has been completed.

1) Thirty days from their successful short sale closing they are able to then purchase another new home, providing they have a credit score of 620 or above (the reporting of a short sale on their credit report drops 40 points average).

CHAPTER 7 Become a Certified Expert

2) One year if they have medical bills on their credit report.

3) Two years if they are applying for a Federal Housing Administration (FHA) loan.

4) Four years if they are applying for a conventional (CONV) Loan.

So, what do I do?
A Short Sale is Truly Your Best Option!

The new program Home Affordable Foreclosure Alternatives (HAFA) helps homeowners not to walk away but sell their home through the new government backed guidelines. National survey finds 40% of borrowers are thinking of abandoning their property. This will save the Lender / Investor from the regular foreclosure action.

We have the green light the public says! 4 in 10 say they will sell and get out. The (HAFA) helps the homeowner with this exit.

A perfect storm! It has never been so easy to get listings.

Do not hang your licenses up. We have the solution with our proven NFSSI™ Short Sale System.

The National Foreclosure Short Sale Institute ≈Certified Expert∆℠ Team of seasoned Real Estate Professionals, Realtors, Brokers, Agents, Attorneys and Title Companies throughout the United States are working together to provide a safe, ethical solution to avoid the pitfalls for homeowners with their short sales and foreclosure problems.

WholesaleProperties.com is a dynamic #1 short sale real estate brokerage, a Florida based company, specializing on the short sale market. Providing in house training and sellers leads with our National Foreclosure Short Sale Institute™.

CHAPTER 7 Become a Certified Expert

NOTES:

Visit our free short sale listing site for buyers and sellers. WholesaleProperties.com and National Foreclosure Short Sales Institute. NFSSICE.com

Short sales were almost unheard of and yet today they have become a new "Tradition".

Nationally recognized, the prestigious NFSSI "Certified Expert"SM is awarded to professionals who want to help homeowners in who are in financial distress and Underwater. Homeowners are in real danger due to the tough economic times. With our proven system, they have a plan of attack.

Our system allows you to increase your listing and quadruple your commissions with our Sellers Package.

Realtor, Broker and Agents that are not certified in this new way of doing business are likely to get a cold shoulder from the Lender / Investor. The Lender / Investor understands that the person processing a Short Sale needs to be a seasoned professional. They now are recognizing and embracing the logo and credentials of National Foreclosure Short Sale Institute "Certified Experts"SM graduates. Lenders have experienced a professional approach and successful transactions. BRAND YOURSELF!

Coaching, support and education is our full-time business. You will not be alone through this process!

How To Create Your Income Stream

1) Two listings a week give you eight listings a month

2) Closing 50% Equals = 4 closing sales (average sale $200,000)

3) 6% commission on an $200,000 sale with a split of 50/50 is $6,000 to the Listing Agent per transaction

CHAPTER 7 Become a Certified Expert

NOTES:

4) At 4 closings with the average commission of $6,000 equals $24,000 for that month.

5) Paying a Coordinator / Processor a 20% fee of the listing commission will give you $19,000 a month.

6) Having a Coordinator / Processor will give you more time to set new listing appointments.

7) Averaging only 1 additional listing per week = 4 more per month.

8) 8 and 4 equals 12 (closing 50% of sales) = 6 sales @ average sale of $200,000 - $36,000 in closing commissions.

9) Paying a Coordinator / Processor 20% fee of the listing commission will give you $28,800 a month.

10) Bonus: The National Association of Realtors survey says: "40% of the leads that are calling from your sign are buyers".

11) Add to your income stream

12) Share your short sale leads with a Buyer's Agent. Build a relationship of understanding that the commission split on the Buyers side will be 60/40.

13) At the rate of 40%, your commission will increase approximately $14,400 of additional income on 6 sales per month.

14) 6 sales per month at $28,800 on the listing side, $14,400 on the buyer's side, equals $43,200.

Utilize your NFSSI "Certified Expert"SM resources and tools:
- Online State of the Art Software Management
- Step by Step Documentation collection
- Underwriting submission
- Negotiating Log
- Closing (HUD)
- Authorized use of all NFSSICE.com materials for duplication.

CHAPTER 7 Become a Certified Expert

NOTES:

- Brand yourself with the seller's package.
- Effective marketing material to customize your personal information
- New law updates
- Coaching Support
- Se Habla Espanol
- Continuing Education
- Networking
- Webinar Seminars
- Short Sale Listing Site (Nationwide)

As serious investors are looking to invest in short sale properties, our highly successful national listing service WholesaleProperties.com for buyers and sellers has attractively priced properties by motivated sellers. This is a great marketing tool for your sellers.

- WholesaleProperties.com Products and Services to Run and Promote your business
- Newsletter, to keep you abreast of our turbulent times and Market Trends
- Legislation
- Statistics
- Foreclosure documentation Service, MyForeclosureDocs.com
- Keep the seller informed to the critical status of the documents from the foreclosure case file to inform all parties.

CC Seller

CC Agent

CC Broker

CC Attorney

CC Coordinator / Processor

- Our national website enhanced by Google is a referral for our team members
- Find a NFSSI ≈Certified Expert∆^{SM}
- NFSSICE.com
- WholesaleProperties.com
- Our Referral Network
- Team Members represent the best of the Industries
- They are the TOP Producers for Success

Chapter 8

Borrower's Options

BORROWER'S OPTIONS

8.1 Foreclosure

If you do nothing... Your Lender will or has already filed foreclosure action against you, and eventually attempt to sell your home at a sheriff sale, where they will not receive anywhere close to what you owe on the property. The lender has the option and may sue you and obtained a deficiency judgement for the difference between the total amount that was owed (including fees) and the amount they were able to sell it for. You will have a completed foreclosure on your credit report for 10 years or more and will not be able to buy another home with conventional financing for MANY years.

"Borrower loses their property to the Lender / Investor".

Going through the foreclosure can knock 200 points off a FICO score, five times as much as the penalty for a short sale.

The reporting of a short sale on their credit report drops 40 points average.

8.2 Loan Modification

If your Lender grants you a modification after many months of deliberating, they will take the amount you are behind and add it to the balance (This puts you further behind since you probably ALREADY owe more on the house then it is worth). If you are lucky, they will drop your interest rates a couple of points. However, due to the amount they put back on to your balance, your saving will not be very significant. A study from the mortgage association of modified loans showed that close to 90% of the homeowner were in foreclosure again within two years.

"Borrower stays in their property".

8.3 Deed in Lieu of Foreclosure

The bank still may have the right to pursue for a deficiency judgment and if you have a second mortgage, they will most likely not agree unless you sign a promissory note for the balance. You still must pay the second mortgage!!! This will also have a very negative impact on your credit rating!

"Lender / Investor receives ownership of property".

(The deficiency does not apply in California, Minnesota, Mississippi, Montana, North Dakota and West Virginia)

8.4 Mortgage Reinstatement

Borrower wants to stay in the property. Borrower wants to get current and reinstate the mortgage. Borrower request for monies owed in the rear and reinstatement letter from the Lender / Investor.

Borrower sends a wire transfer or certified funds to the Lender / Investor. Upon receipt of acknowledgement of funds, the Lender / Investor sends reinstatement documentation.

8.5 Forbearance

Borrower wants to stay in their property. Borrower acknowledges there was a temporary hardship and was not able to pay their mortgage payment. The Lender / Investor negotiated with the Borrower for missed payments and legal fees to reinstate the mortgage.

The Lender / Investor agrees to the following conditions for the Borrower to pay over a period of time at the end of the scheduled loan amortization or the Borrower will be given a period of time in which to pay delinquencies.

8.6 SHORT SALE / ACCEPTABLE HARDSHIPS

A principle borrowers or co-borrower must have one of the following 1 - 22 to qualify for a short sale.

The borrower must demonstrate a financial hardship in order for a Lender / Investor to accept a short sale.

A short sale is when a Lender / Investor will take less that what is owed on the mortgage of the borrower.

Financial insolvency is the most common hardship due to the sub-prime crisis.

The principle borrower's letter of hardship is in their own handwriting and will allow the financial Lender / Investor to consider the hardship along with their financial statements.

This option called the new "Tradition" short sale is allowing the Lender / Investor to minimize their losses verses the foreclosure process. The Mortgage Bankers Association says that the Lender / Investor will save 15% in losses by doing the short sale verses a foreclosure. The average cost to the Lender / Investor on a foreclosure is $44,000 as the short sale is less at $21,000. This is why the Lender / Investor is willing to take a short sale.

1) DEATH OF PRINCIPAL BORROWER

The principle borrower signed on the mortgage and the promissory note. A co-borrower is now left in a position of no additional income to make said mortgage payment.

2) DEATH OF PRINCIPAL BORROWER FAMILY MEMBER

The principle borrower relied on the additional income to make the full payment of the mortgage.

3) SERIOUS ILLNESS OF PRINCIPAL BORROWER

The principle borrower stopped working due to an illness and medical expenses where there was no income or any other household wage earner to pay the mortgage.

4) SERIOUS ILLNESS OF PRINCIPAL BORROWER»S FAMILY MEMBER

The principle borrower's additional household wage earner that contributed to the mortgage payment stopped working due to illness and medical expenses.

5) MARITAL PROBLEMS (DIVORCE, SEPARATION)

When two household wage earners relied on both incomes to make the mortgage payment, depending upon the outcome of the separation or divorce many times during the process they are maintaining two house-holds.

6) UNEMPLOYMENT

The principle borrower lost his/her employment with or without notice, as most Americans are living from pay check to paycheck.

7) LESSENED INCOME

The principle borrower that relied on a current income had a reduction in wages.

CHAPTER 8 Borrowers Options

8) PROPERTY ABANDONMENT

The principle borrower vacated the premises due to (examples) hurricane, flood, natural disaster or unlivable conditions.

9) EXCESSIVE OBLIGATIONS

The principle borrower current mortgage was a sub-prime loan and it adjusted along with the cost of the living expenses accelerated along with the increase of flood, wind and fire insurance and real estate taxes.

10) LONG DISTANCE EMPLOYMENT TRANSFER

The principle borrower was notified from his employer that his employment was no longer needed at his current location, they relocated him over 100 miles or more to a different location.

11) MILITARY SERVICE

The principle borrower is in the military and their time of duty was extended. The "Serviceperson Civil Relief Act (SCRAM)" provides specific details.

12) UNABLE TO SELL PROPERTY

The principle borrowers' mortgage is higher than the market value of the property.

13) UNABLE TO RENT THE PROPERTY

The principle borrower is unable to rent the property because his mortgage payments are higher than what he can rent it for and does not have the income to subsides the difference.

14) LOSS DUE TO ACCIDENT, FIRE OR NATURAL CAUSES

The principle borrower did not have insurance or it was not sufficient to cover his losses.

15) FRAUD

The principle borrower invested in an investment and was unable to get his principle due to illegal activities.

16) SERVICING PROBLEMS (ARM)

The principle borrowers were in an Adjustable Rate Mortgage (ARM) sub-prime loan, the mortgage payment adjusted to a higher amount. The borrower's income did not increase to the higher payment.

17) INCARCERATION

The principle borrower or co-borrower is in a Federal, State or County Correctional Institution. Due to the circumstances there is no income mortgage payment.

18) PAYMENT DISPUTE

The principle borrowers' amount on the mortgage is different than the amount on the mortgage note.

19) IMPOSED COST (ENERGY/ENVIRONMENT)

The principle borrower's property taxes increased from an energy/environment catastrophe. The property owner had a fixed income.

20) INCURABLE PROPERTY PROBLEMS

The principle borrowers living conditions drinking water, pollution sink hole.

21) OWNERSHIP TRANSFER PENDING

The principle borrowers title deficiencies.

22) PRINCIPLE BORROWER HAS BUSINESS FAILURE

The principle borrower income came from owning his own business, the business failure caused his inability to pay the mortgage.

Chapter 9

Seller's Package

CHAPTER 9 Seller's Package

NOTES:

SELLER'S PACKAGE
Realtor, Broker and Agent

See samples (22A, 22B, and 22C) of cover letters introducing yourself and your services. You need to insert the letter into your Seller's Package.

"The cover of the Seller's Package brands your identity, name and brokerage firm".

The forms and documents used in this manual have been approved by the Florida Association of Realtors® and the Florida Bar Association for Florida (FAR/BAR) use only.

You need to contact your states' Real Estate Association Board of Realtors for your forms and documents.

(If you are Agent with a Brokerage Firm/Broker typically they have their own approved required forms and documents.)

9.1 Financial Statements (choose one)

A) Housing Urban Development HUD - Form #92417
(4 pages)

The sample (1A) is the long form used when the Seller / Borrower has multiple properties, financial and personal assets.

B) Freddie Mac Form #1126 (3 pages)

The sample (1B) is the short form used when the Seller / Borrower has limited properties, financial and personal assets.

C) Standard (4 Pages)

The sample (1C) is provided by many lenders or their current bookkeeper / accountants.

This form is commonly used with the Seller / Borrower as their primary home and expenses are not extensive.

These forms must be signed by Seller / Borrower.

9.2. Federal Tax Returns

The sample (2A, IRS Form 1040) complete copies of last 2 years or the following (2B IRS Form 4868) copy of extensions.

The sample (2C) is an IRS request for transcript of the tax return, form 4506-T.

This is to be signed copies by the Seller / Borrower.

9.3 Paycheck Stubs or any proof of income (Copies of last 2 months)

The sample (3A) copy of the paycheck/stub, (3B IRS Form W2), or proof of income letter from employer.

CHAPTER 9 Seller's Package

9.4 Bank Accounts (Checking or Savings)

Borrowers must show two (2) months of bank statements. If bank accounts have been closed, show closed statements.

9.5 Disclaimer Seller / Borrower, Listing Agent - Broker documentation.

The sample (4A) is a foreclosure disclaimer agreement.

This is to be signed by the Seller / Borrower only.

9.6 Hardship (22) acceptable terms by Housing Urban Development (HUD)

The sample (5A) needs to be handwritten by the Seller / Borrower (note you can have multiple hardships).

The sample (5A) is a typed template for easy reading.

CHAPTER 9 Seller's Package

NOTES:

SUGGESTIONS:

Keep it to one page

Address it "To Whom It May Concern".

What caused the hardships to not make the mortgage payments?

State that you wanted or attempted to sell your house in order to pay off the mortgage.

However, with the current market conditions and/or condition of the home you are not able to sell it for what is owed.

Upon an offer from the Buyer's Agent do not state the contract price and do not include Buyers name and phone number.

The Seller / Borrower does not include his home phone or cell in hardship letter.

The Borrower shall not give a value on the property. State that you have a real estate agent handling the listing.

This must be signed by Seller / Borrower.

9.7 SHORT SALE / ACCEPTABLE HARDSHIPS

A principle borrower or co-borrower must have one of the following H1-22 to qualify for a short sale.

The borrower must demonstrate a financial hardship in order for a Lender / Investor to accept a short sale.

A short sale is when a Lender / Investor will take less than what is owed on the mortgage of the borrower.

Financial insolvency is the most common hardship due to the sub-prime crisis.

The principle borrower's letter of hardship is in their own handwriting and will allow the financial Lender / Investor to consider the hardship along with their financial statements.

This option called the new "Tradition" short sale is allowing the Lender / Investor to minimize their losses verses the foreclosure process. The Mortgage Bankers Association says that the Lender / Investor will save 15% in losses by doing the short sale verses a foreclosure. The average cost to the Lender / Investor on a foreclosure is $44,000 as the short sale is less at $21,000. This is why the Lender / Investor is willing to take a short sale.

H1) DEATH OF PRINCIPAL BORROWER

H2) DEATH OF PRINCIPAL BORROWER FAMILY MEMBER

H3) SERIOUS ILLNESS OF PRINCIPAL BORROWER

H4) SERIOUS ILLNESS OF PRINCIPAL BORROWER'S FAMILY MEMBER

H5) MARITAL PROBLEMS (DIVORCE, SEPARATION)

H6) UNEMPLOYMENT

H7) LESSENED INCOME

H8) PROPERTY ABANDONMENT

H9) EXCESSIVE OBLIGATIONS

H10) LONG DISTANCE EMPLOYMENT TRANSFER

H11) MILITARY SERVICE

H12) UNABLE TO SELL PROPERTY

H13) UNABLE TO RENT THE PROPERTY

H14) LOSS DUE TO ACCIDENT, FIRE OR NATURAL CAUSES

H15) FRAUD

NOTES:

H16) SERVICING PROBLEMS (ARM)

H17) INCARCERATION

H18) PAYMENT DISPUTE

H19) IMPOSED COST (ENERGY / ENVIRONMENT)

H20) INCURABLE PROPERTY PROBLEMS

H21) OWNERSHIP TRANSFER PENDING

H22) PRINCIPLE BORROWER HAS BUSINESS FAILURE

CHAPTER 9 Seller's Package

9.8 Authorization to Release Information

For the following parties: Broker / Agent, Coordinator / Processor, Title Company and Attorney.

See the sample (6A) is the document that designed to be used for up to three Service / Lender / Investors loans.

(see monthly mortgage statement or letters for Lenders name, loan number and Lender's phone)

Once the Servicer / Lender / Investor acknowledges you, as a party to the "Authorization to Release Information" this will expedite accurate information regarding the Sellers/Borrowers mortgage.

This is signed by the Borrower and or Co-Borrower only.

9.9 Exclusive Right of Sale Listing Agreement / transaction broker (ERST-14th)

The sample (7A) is a listing agreement (4 pages).

This is to be signed by the Seller and Agent.

9.10 Short Sale Addendum to Exclusive Right of Sale Listing

CHAPTER 9 Seller's Package

NOTES:

Agreement (ERSA-1)

The sample (8A) is a short sale addendum.

To be signed by the Seller only.

10. Modification to Listing Agreement (MLA-3)
(property price change)

The sample (9A) used as is a price change form.

Warning: DO NOT change the price on Multiple Listing without the Seller's signature.

This is signed by the Seller only.

9.12 Seller / Borrower Non-Performance Addendum

This addendum used in this short sale must be approved by the Brokerage Firm / Broker.

The sample (12A) is a listing agreement addendum.

This is when the seller does not comply to the agreements and documents signed to perform the listing agents fiduciaries duties.

To be signed Seller / Borrower. (This must be completed in 7-14 days)

9.13 Arm's Length Transaction. This may be requested by the Servicer / Lender / Investor to be signed by all parties to the transaction. See Sample (13A)

9.14A Property Analysis Form This form is an inspection and repair estimate sheet to send to the Servicer / Lender / Investor. Informing them of the condition of the property. See Sample (14A)

9.14B Photo Log This log of the photos you supply to the Servicer / Lender / Investor See Sample (14B)

9.15 Check List of 1 - 14 Seller / Borrower

- 1) Financial Statements
- 2) Federal Tax Returns
- 3) Paycheck Stubs or Any Proof of Income
- 4) Bank Statements
- 5) Disclaimer Documentation Seller / Borrower Listing Broker / Agent
- 6) Hardship Letter from Seller / Borrower
- 7) Authorization to Release Information
- 8) Exclusive Right of Sale Listing Agreement
- 9) Short Sale Addendum to Exclusive Right of Sale Listing Agreement
- 10) Modification to Listing Agreement (Use for Price Change)
- 11) Seller / Borrower Listing Agreement Addendum
- 12) Arm's Length
- 13) Property Analysis Form
- 14) Photo Log

CHAPTER 9 Seller's Package

NOTES:

Chapter 10

Coordinator / Processing Services

COORDINATOR / PROCESSING SERVICES

Coordinator / Processor that are not certified in this new traditional way of doing business are likely to get a cold shoulder from the Lender/Investor. As the Lender / Investor understands that the person processing is a seasoned professional and they now are embracing certified experts as shown from their transmissions with the NFSSI "Certified Expert"^{SM} initials and logo.

Nationally recognized, the prestigious National Foreclosure Short Sale Institute "Certified Expert"^{SM} is awarded to professionals who want to help homeowners who are in financial stress and underwater. They are in real danger due to the tough economic times; with our proven systems they have a plan of attack.

Short sales are not all the same with our proven system and coaching you will have advanced knowledge to close your sales.

In addition to all the services of National Foreclosure Short Sale Institute "Certified Expert"^{SM}, you will be able to keep abreast of the critical status of documents from the foreclosure case. Monitor by the services of www.myforeclosuredocs.com.

Processing a short sale and taking the listing takes a tremendous amount of detail. To facilitate a short sale, you spend a lot of down time holding to talk to a Servicer / Lender / Investor's representative and getting the necessary documents to them over and over.

Once you reach the Seller / Lender's representative you may find that after spending considerable time and sacrificing your work hours that you were informed, they do not own the mortgage and they have assigned the mortgage to a new Servicer / Lender / Investor. Then you must start the process all over again. Or the Servicer / Lender / Investor is handling the shorts sale and it still needs to get authorized by the Lender / Investor who is the true holder of the note.

CHAPTER 10 Coordinator / Processing Services

NFSSICE.com provides a proven comprehensive state by state seller package to educate and facilitate the process for win-win results. With our highly designed software is state of the art tracking for comprehensive reporting for our team, sellers and buyers. With this you can initiate a jump start to success. It is critical that you know the process for a successful seller closing.

The following functions are compiled by the Realtor, Broker / Agent for the Seller / Borrower:

- Sellers Contract (As Is)
- Short Sale Addendum
- Proof of Funds/Buyers Lender Pre-qualification Letter
- Listing Agreement
- Modification to the Listing Agreement
- Preliminary HUD (Housing and Urban Development)
- Hardship Letter
- Financial Statement
- Comparative Market Analyst (CMA)
- Proof of Sellers Income Tax Returns for the prior two years
- Authorization to release information to the Agent / Processor / Attorney

The following checklist is for the submission of the Short Sale Package to the Servicer / Lender / Investor for a successful result:

- 1. Fax Cover Sheet See Sample (23B)
- 2. Lender/Investor Cover Letter (Overview of Offer)
- 3. (HUD #1) Preliminary Settlement Statement

This document is prepared by the title company from the contract, for the Lender / Investor to show their net proceeds from the sale.

- 4. "As Is" Contract for Sale and Purchase
- 5. Short Sale Addendum to Purchase and Sale Contract
- 6. (FHA) Disclosure)

This document is used when the Buyer has been approved for an (FHA) loan program.

CHAPTER 10 Coordinator / Processing Services

NOTES:

- 7. Copy of the Deposit / Escrow Check
- 8. Proof of Funds - Bank Statement (When there is a cash offer from the Buyer)
- 9. Financing, a Pre-Qualifying letter from the Buyer's Lender
- 10. Authorization to Release Information
- 11. Hardship Letter Handwritten by Seller / Borrower
- 12. Financial Statements
- 13. Paycheck Stubs or any proof of income (Copies of last 2 months)
- 14. Bank Statement, Seller / Borrower (Last 2 Months)
- 15. Federal Tax Return (Complete copies of last 2 years, or copy of extension)
- 16. Arm's Length Transaction
- 17. Exclusive Right of Sale Listing Agreement
- 18 Short Sale Addendum to Exclusive Right of Sale Listing Agreement
- 19. Property Analysis Form and Photo Log
- 20. Multiple Listing Service (MLS) The current listing of subject property.
- 21. Multiple Listing Service (MLS) Price History of the subject property
- 22. Multiple Listing Service (MLS) Competitive Market Analysis

Submitting the Lender / Investor Package for Conditions and Approval

The authorization to release information should have been sent into the Servicer / Lender / Investor already, if not do this NOW! (see page 102 - Authorization to Release Information in this manual)

Contact the Servicer / Lender / Investor to give you the fax number or email where to send the short sale package.

They are referring you to the representative of the:

A) Short Sale Department
B) Loss Mitigation Department
C) Work Out Department
D) Liquidation Department
E) Correspondence Department

CHAPTER 10 Coordinator / Processing Services

NOTES:

The representative may inform you that the mortgage may have been sold / assigned to a new Servicer / Lender / Investor and you may need to re-fax the Authorization to Release Information Form to a new number.

Add to the short sale package a fax cover sheet.

Include the Borrower, Loan Number, Property Address and your name and contact information.

Fax or Email your short sale package in for conditions and approval.

The National Foreclosure Short Sale Institute "Certified Experts"^{SM} Team of season real estate professionals, Realtors, Brokers and agents, Coordinator / Processor, Attorneys and Title Company Professionals throughout the United States are working together to provide a safe, ethical solution to foreclosure issues to avoid the pitfalls for homeowners with their short sales and foreclosure problems.

Chapter 11

Jump Start Your Wholesaling Business Now!

CHAPTER 11   Jump Start Your Wholesaling Business Now!

NOTES:

JUMP START YOUR WHOLESALING BUSINESS NOW

Realtor / Broker / Agent

Now that you have received the course manual study it thoroughly, you can begin your own National Foreclosure Short Sale business right away, without delay, and be a "Certified Expert".

Concentrate on the material. Read it twice for meaning and understanding of the process of the Seller / Borrower package and the Coordinator / Processor / Lender / Investor package. Study the packages and process until it is seared into your soul.

The licensed salesperson responsibilities, before you try and help the property owner in default a Real Estate Professional should advise the property owner in writing. Consult a real estate attorney for all legal advice and consult with a certified public accountant (CPA) for tax advice.

In any other state than Florida, you need to contact your State Association Board of Realtors for your forms and documents.

(If you are an Agent with a Brokerage Firm / Broker typically have their own approved required forms and documents.)

The following are the types of opportunities to obtain your listings leads so you can soar to new levels of success in the new "Tradition" of short sales:

1. **REFERRAL**

The referral is the most prestigious type of listing lead because it is a testimonial to your success.

CHAPTER 11 Jump Start Your Wholesaling Business Now!

NOTES:

2. SIGNAGE

40% of all sales transactions come from the properties "FOR SALE" sign. The party calling regarding the subject property, may not be interested in that property, but maybe interested in listing their property with you because of your visible sign in the neighborhood.

3. A WALK-IN

Some brokerage requirements have floor duties, this is a great opportunity to get a listing or sell a home to parties as they are interested and motivated.

4. OPEN HOUSE

This draws great attention, as the neighborhood is being alerted for prospective buyers and sellers, to take an opportunity to see what is in the marketplace. Realtor, Broker / Agents will also take opportunity to bring their clients.

5. THE INTERNET

The Internet is a great tool to market yourself. Marketing through your personal website educates various options for the homeowner. Agents who want to maintain their competitive edge will need to become familiar with the ever growing array of online consumer home-buying tools, broaden their online presence, and enhance their communication with clients through the use of the latest Web trends such as blogs, social media sites, and podcasts.

6. ADVERTISING

Sending a postcard to the area in which the subject property is located alerts the present homeowners of the availability of what is on the market and brands yourself in that neighborhood.

7. PENDING FORECLOSURE NOTICE / ACTIONS

Obtaining these notices / actions from the courthouse public records or the local newspapers give you endless leads. See sample on next 2 pages.

8. SEMINAR

Using a press release in your local news organizations will promote your skills to the struggling homeowners and underwater owners that focus on avoiding foreclosure this will draw crowds (See sample on next 2 pages).

9. SELLER'S PACKAGE

The seller package, brands you as a National Foreclosure Short Sale Institute "Certified Expert"SM has been created to inform the homeowner of alternatives to this mortgage crisis. This is offered free of charge to the homeowner that needs to have alternative options.

GET STARTED / STEP BY STEP

A) Branding and Marketing Yourself

See Samples of Press Releases in the Real Estate forms booklet.

The following tools, marketing information and tactics we provide are for a win-win solution for the short sale campaign.

The goals of this program for a licensed Real Estate Person are to start you off branding yourself with your photo on the informative Seller / Borrowers package, which is offered free to the Seller / Borrower that is in the foreclosure process or to the financial hardships that have occurred.

CHAPTER 11 Jump Start Your Wholesaling Business Now!

NOTES:

Notice of Action

IN THE CIRCUIT COURT OF THE SEVENTEENTH JUDICIAL CIRCUIT IN AND FOR BROWARD COUNTY, FLORIDA CIVIL DIVISION Case No. 91-08361-25

BANCBOSTON MORTGAGE CORPORATION, a Florida corporation, etc.,
Plaintiff.
v.
KIETH A. HAALAND a/k/a KEITH A. HAALAND, et al.,
Defendants,
TO: The unknown heirs, devisees, creditors, or other parties claiming by, through, under or against Defendant, Beverly A. Haaland, a/k/a Beverly Ann Haaland, deceased.
YOU ARE NOTIFIED that an action to foreclose a mortgage on the following property in Broward County, Florida:
LOT 11, IN BLOCK 3, OF Pearl estates, according to the Plat thereof, as recorded in Plant Book 40, at Page 42, of the Public Records of Broward County, Florida. had been filed against you and you are required to serve a copy of your written defenses, if any, to it on Mindy C. Funk, Esquire, Rosenthal & Yarchin, CenTrust Financial Center, Suite 2300, 100 Southeast 2nd Street, Miami, Florida 33131-2198, on or before June 3rd 1991 and to file the original with the Clerk of this Court either before service on Plaintiff's attorneys or immediately thereafter; otherwise, a default will be entered against you for the relief demanded in the Complaint.
WITNESS my hand and seal of this Court on APR 18, 1991.
ROBERT E. LOCKWOOD, Clerk TRUE COPY Circuit Court Seal By: ALICE PHILPS, Deputy Clerk, Mindy C. Funk, Esquire Rosenthal & Yarchin CenTrust Financial Center Suite 2300 100 Southeast 2nd Street, Miami, Florida 33131-2198, Telephone: (305) 374-6600 4/23-30 5/7-14 B91-M-042367

Notice of Sale

IN THE CIRCUIT COURT OF THE SEVENTEENTH JUDICIAL CIRCUIT IN AND FOR BROWARD COUNTY, FLORIDA CIVIL DIVISION Case No. 91-08361-25 BANCBOSTON MORTGAGE CORPORATION, a Florida corporation, etc., Plaintiff v. KIETH A. HAALAND, a/k/a KEITH A. HAALAND, et al., Defendants, NOTICE IS HEREBY given that under and by virtue of the Summary Final Judgment of Foreclosure dated July 2, 1991, and entered in Case No. 91-0836-25, by the Court in the above-styled cause, the undersigned Clerk of the Court will sell at public auction to the highest bidder for cash or cashier's check in the lobby of the Broward County Courthouse, 201 S.E. 6th Street, Fort Lauderdale, Florida, at 11:00 a.m., on August 19, 1991, the property described below:
Lot 11, in Block 3, of PEARL ESTATES, according to the Plat thereof, as recorded in Plat book 40, at Page 42, of the Public Records of Broward County, Florida. DATED this 3rd day of July, 1991.
ROBERT E. LOCKWOOD, Clerk A TRUE COPY Circuit Court Seal By: THOMAS WILLIAMS, Deputy Clerk Alan Rosenthal, Esquire Rosenthal & Yarchin Suite 2300 CenTrust Financial Center 100 Southeast 2nd Street Miami, Florida 33131-2198 Telephone: (305) 374-6600
7/8-15 B91-F-070828

Notice of Action comes approximately four (4) weeks after the first notice and is paid by the Plaintiff to continue legal proceedings to the Final Sale.

Notice of Sale which is also published in the legal paper is paid for by the plaintiff and published following the Final Judgement and Order by the Judge to proceed with the sale of the property.

LEGAL PUBLIC NOTICES:

The charges and costs of the total legal process of the foreclosure would be in the final judgment of all monies owed on the said property. The property owner or the bidder who is purchasing the property at the sale would be paying those charges, they are all included in the final judgement.

If the lender received the property back fees and charges of the foreclosure process are costs to the lender.

NEW FORECLOSURE CASES FILED

FIRST NOTICES OF FORECLOSURE CASES FILED. INFORMATION INCLUDES CASE NUMBER, PLAINTIFF, DEFENDANT, PLAT BOOK AND PAGE NUMBER FOR FURTHER SEARCH OF THE PROPERTY. WHEN AVAILABLE, THE PHYSICAL ADDRESS, AMOUNT OWED, ASSESSED VALUE AND THE NAME OF THE PLAINTIFF'S ATTORNEY.

■ 9 1-08361-25BANCBOSTON MORTGAGE CORPORATION, vs: KEITH A. HAALAND, mtg:$27,205.42, 8.5%, Lt 11, Blk 3 PEARL ESTATES, PB 40/42 BROWARD COUNTY, 3516 S. W. 14th Street, Ft. Lauderdale FL ass'd val $52,020.00 Barry s. Yarchin, Esq. (305) 374-6600

New Case Notice / Complaint for Foreclosure, printed in a legal newspaper as the Complaint gets filed the following day. This is the most important one because this notice informs that this is a troubled property. You need to get this information from the start.

CHAPTER 11 Jump Start Your Wholesaling Business Now!

NOTES:

The individual package brands you as a "Certified Expert".

B) Preparing for Your Listing Appointment.

The following are necessary to guide you for a successful listing appointment:

1) You should print the subject's property tax card from the Multiple Listing Service (MLS).

The reason why you are doing this is verifying the party or parties you are having the listing appointment with is in title. Note, if there are additional parties, they need to be at the listing appointment. All parties of interest need to agree to sell the property.

2) The Multiple Listing Service (MLS) has a feature for pulling the subjects property history.

That function will give you:

A) If the subject property is on the market and listed with an agent.

B) When the property was purchased.

C) The original prices since the history data was collected.

D) Mortgage is separate information. It shows the original lender, the mortgage amount and date. The parties to the said mortgage, additional documentation for financial information, must be required for an authorization from the borrower, to the lender.

E) If the Mortgagor / Lender is the Mortgage Electronic Registration System (MERS), and you review the recorded mortgage either in the public record or from the Borrower / Seller, you can obtain the 18-digit MERS number located in the upper right-hand corner on the first page of the mortgage. Enter the MERS number at:
https://www.mer-servicerid.org/sis/
to get information on the mortgage servicer.

Other than the Mortgage Electronic Registration System (MERS) number, most other Servicer / Lender information will be found in the public records.

1)   If the foreclosure is in progress you can pull these documents up through Internet access.

2)   If the foreclosure is in the beginning stages or parties have just been served then the mortgage documents will be attached to the legal action.

If the Borrower does not have this information, these are the following steps at the listing appointment:

The Borrower may have a current closing package for your review. These documentations will provide, you an insight of the Borrowers position.

If the Borrower has not been notified of an action, ask the Borrower for all the corresponding documents that have been sent by the Lender.

Comparative Market Analysis (CMA)

You need to prepare yourself a market price on the subject property.

Consider the following types of property, active and sold:

    a)   Bank owned

    b)   Short Sales

    c)   A distressed house in need of repair

    d)   Properties that are not in hardship

C)   *Listing Appointment / Sellers Package*

All listing appointments are not all the same.

You must qualify your homeowner. If you do not qualify your homeowner it may be difficult to move forward.

This is not your normal listing, setting more realistic expectations on the homeowner's sale price.

The homeowner is doing very little shopping for a listing agent, if any at all, as the homeowner is unconformable in explaining the situation they are in.

This is a win - win listing appointment.

This is an absolute requirement to your valuable time in your business, time is money.

Each one has its own challenges for the homeowner.

On this appointment you must show compassion regardless of their situation, as the homeowner is in a stressful situation.

You want to be informative about the process, as your sellers package makes the process complete.

Remember, if your homeowner is not responding to your request this could be challenging. The Seller / Borrower needs to be cooperative.

Your homeowner must be totally committed in working with you, this is an absolute must, or you must move on. See following sample Seller / Borrower Non-Performance Addendum (12-A).

Your biggest challenge is the homeowner overcoming the misinformation from the news media, friends and family on the short sale process.

As this process is giving them an opportunity to avoid a foreclosure and with your expertise you can help solve their crisis and provide with positive results.

The guidance that you as a NFSSICE "Certified Expert"SM, will give will enable the Seller will see the potential way out of their hardship, and it will motivate them to be very involved in the process.

1) Serious Questions for The Seller's (Asked By Listing Agent)

A) The Borrowers considering bankruptcy. If so, they need to consult an Attorney prior to signing a listing agreement?

B) Do they have any current law suits that they have not responded to as these become judgments and will "cloud" the title of the property unless negotiated with the lien holders.

C) Have they received any letter or correspondence from the Servicer / Lender / Investor on the Housing Affordable Foreclosure Alternative (HAFA) program? What date did they receive it? They have 14 days to respond to that government program for their primary residence.

CHAPTER 11   Jump Start Your Wholesaling Business Now!

D) Are their plans to reside in their primary property while they do a short sale.

If relocating, how soon must they move?

E)   Do you hold a security clearance?

A security clearance is a status granted to individuals allowing them access to classified information or to restricted areas.

The following must take serious action and you must speak to your supervisors:

      1)   You are in the military

      2)   You are in law enforcement

      3)   You are in civilian's

F) Have they pulled any permits from the state, county or city for the property?

If so, have them provide the documents.

If permits have not been finalized take that in consideration of cost.

G) Are the Seller / Borrowers currently in any legal litigation?

If so, provide the

If there are any current liens, please provide the documents.

H) Do they understand that a Home Equity Line of Credit (HELOC) is a lien on their property?

The Servicer / Lender / Investor may require the Seller / Borrower to sign a Promissory Note to pay the balance before they release the lien.

CHAPTER 11 Jump Start Your Wholesaling Business Now!

C 2) SELLER'S PACKAGE

Realtor, Broker and Agent

See the following sample of a cover letter introducing yourself and your services. You need to insert the letter into your Sellers Package.

"The cover of the Sellers Package Brands your identity, name and brokerage firm.".

The forms and documents used in this manual have been approved by the Florida Association of Realtors and the Florida Bar Association for Florida (FAR / BAR) use only.

In any other state than Florida, you need to contact your States Association Board of Realtors for your forms and documents.

(If you are Agent with a Brokerage Firm / Broker typically they have their own approved required forms and documents.)

1. Financial Statements (choose one)

A) Housing Urban Development (HUD) Financial-Form #92417 (4 pages)

The following sample (1A) is the long form used when the Seller / Borrower has multiple properties, financial and personal assets.

B) Freddie Mac Financial Form #1126 (3 pages)

The following sample (1B) is the short form used when the Seller / Borrower has limited properties, financial and personal assets.

C) Standard (1 Page)

The following sample (1C) is provided by many lenders or their current bookkeeper / accountants.

This form is commonly used with the Seller / Borrower as their primary home and expenses are not extensive.

These forms must be signed by Seller / Borrower

2. Federal Tax Returns

The following samples (2A) complete copies of last 2 years or the (2B) copy of extensions.

IRS Request for Transcript of Tax Return, Form 4506-T. The Servicer / Lender may request the Seller / Borrower to sign the IRS form in order to receive a transcript of the Seller / Borrower's tax returns. See Sample 2C.

This is to be signed copies by the Seller / Borrower.

3. Paycheck Stubs or any proof of income (Copies of last 2 months)

The following samples (3A) copy of the paycheck / stub or (3B) proof of income a letter (1099).

4. Bank Accounts (Checking or Savings)

Seller / Borrower must show two (2) months of bank statements. If bank accounts are closed, show closed statements.

5. Disclaimer *Seller / Borrower*, Listing agent / Broker documentation.

CHAPTER 11   Jump Start Your Wholesaling Business Now!

NOTES:

The sample (4A) is a confidentiality agreement that you are not engaged in rendering legal or accounting advice and the Seller / Borrower should seek an attorney or CPA - Accountant with any and all questions.

This is to be signed by the Seller / Borrower only.

6. Hardship (22) acceptable terms approved by Housing Urban Development (HUD)

The sample (5A) needs to be handwritten by the Seller / Borrower (note, you can have multiple hardships).

The sample (5B) is a typed template for easy reading.

SUGGESTIONS:

Keep it to one page

Address it ≈To Whom It May Concern∆.

What caused the hardships to not make the mortgage payments?

State that you wanted or attempted to sell your house in order to pay off the mortgage.

However, with the current market conditions and/or condition of the home you are not able to sell it for what is owed.

Upon an offer from the buyer's agent do not state the contract price and do not include Buyers name and phone number.

The Seller / Borrower does not include his home phone or cell in hardship letter.

The Seller / Borrower shall not give a value on the property.

This has to be signed by Seller / Borrower

SHORT SALE / ACCEPTABLE HARDSHIPS

A principle borrower or co-borrower must have at least one of the following 1 - 22 to qualify for a short sale.

The borrower must demonstrate a financial hardship in order for a Lender / Investor to accept a short sale.

A short sale is when a Lender / Investor will take less that what is owed on the mortgage of the borrower.

Financial insolvency is the most common hardship due to the sub-prime crisis.

The principle borrower's letter of hardship is in their own handwriting and will allow the financial Lender / Investor to consider the hardship along with their financial statements.

This option called the new "Tradition" short sale is allowing the Lender / Investor to minimize their losses verses the foreclosure process. The Mortgage Bankers Association says that the Lender / Investor will save 15% in losses by doing the short sale verses a foreclosure. The average cost to the Lender / Investor on a foreclosure is $44,000 as the short sale is less at $21,000. This is why the Lender / Investor is willing to take a short sale.

H1) DEATH OF PRINCIPAL BORROWER

The principle borrower signed on the mortgage and the promissory note. A co-borrower is now left in a position of no additional income to make said mortgage payment.

HH2) DEATH OF PRINCIPAL BORROWER FAMILY MEMBER

The principle borrower relied on the additional income to make the full payment of the mortgage.

H3) SERIOUS ILLNESS OF PRINCIPAL BORROWER

The principle borrower stopped working due to an illness and medical expenses where there was no income or any other household wage earner to pay the mortgage.

H4) SERIOUS ILLNESS OF PRINCIPAL BORROWER»S FAMILY MEMBER

The principle borrower's additional household wage earner that contributed to the mortgage payment stopped working due to illness and medical expenses.

H5) MARITAL PROBLEMS (DIVORCE, SEPARATION)

When two household wage earners relied on both incomes to make the mortgage payment, depending upon the outcome of the separation or divorce many times during the process they are maintaining two house- holds.

H6) UNEMPLOYMENT

The principle borrower lost his / her employment with or without notice, as most Americans are living from paycheck to paycheck.

H7) LESSENED INCOME

The principle borrower that relied on a current income had a reduction in wages.

H8) PROPERTY ABANDONMENT

The principle borrower vacated the premises due to (examples) hurricane, flood, natural disaster or unlivable conditions.

H9) EXCESSIVE OBLIGATIONS

The principle borrowers' current mortgage was a sub-prime loan and it is adjusted along with the cost of the living expenses accelerated along with the increase of flood, wind and fire insurance and real estate taxes.

H10) LONG DISTANCE EMPLOYMENT TRANSFER

The principle borrower was notified from his employer that his employment was no longer needed at his current location, they relocated him over 100 miles or more to a different location.

H11) MILITARY SERVICE

The principle borrower is in the military and their time of duty was extended. The ≈Serviceperson Civil Relief Act (SCRAM)∆ provides specific details.

H12) UNABLE TO SELL PROPERTY

The principle borrowers' mortgage is higher than the market value of the property.

H13) UNABLE TO RENT THE PROPERTY

The principle borrower is unable to rent the property because his mortgage payments are higher than what he can rent it for and does not have the income to subsides the difference.

H14) LOSS DUE TO ACCIDENT, FIRE OR NATURAL CAUSES

The principle borrower did not have insurance, or it was not sufficient to cover his losses.

H15) FRAUD

The principle borrower invested in an investment that went bad due to fraudulent activities, and was unable to get his principle back due to illegal activities.

H16) SERVICING PROBLEMS (ARM)

The principle borrowers were in an Adjustable Rate Mortgage (ARM), sub-prime loan, the mortgage payment adjusted to a higher amount. The borrower's income did not increase to the higher payment.

H17) INCARCERATION

The principle borrower or co-borrower is in a Federal, State or County Correctional Institution. Due to the circumstances there is no income for the mortgage payment.

H18) PAYMENT DISPUTE

The principle borrowers' amount on the mortgage is different than the amount on the mortgage note.

H19) IMPOSED COST (ENERGY / ENVIRONMENT)

The principle borrower's property taxes increased from an energy / environment catastrophe. The property owner had a fixed income.

H20) INCURABLE PROPERTY PROBLEMS

The principle borrowers living conditions. example pollution of drinking water, sink hole, etc.

CHAPTER 11 Jump Start Your Wholesaling Business Now!

H21) OWNERSHIP TRANSFER PENDING

The principle borrowers have title deficiencies.

H22) PRINCIPLE BORROWER HAS BUSINESS FAILURE

The principle borrower's income came from owning his own business, the business failed and caused the inability to pay the mortgage.

---

7. Authorization to Release Information

For the following parties: Broker / Agent, Coordinator / Processor, Title Company and Attorney. To be authorized to speak to the Servicer / Lender / Investor.

See the sample (6A) is the document that designed to be used for up to three Service / Lender / Investors loans.

(see monthly mortgage statement or letters for Lenders name, loan number and Lender's phone)

Once the Servicer / Lender / Investor acknowledges you, as a party to the "Authorization to Release Information" this will expedite accurate information regarding the Seller's / Borrower's mortgage.

This is signed by the Borrower and or Co-Borrower only.

8. Exclusive Right of Sale Listing Agreement / transaction Broker (ERST - 14th)

The sample (7A) is a listing agreement (3 pages).

This is to be signed by the Seller and Listing Agent, Pertinent to the listing.

9. Short Sale addendum to Exclusive Right of Sale Listing Agreement (ERSA - 1)

The sample (8A) is a short sale addendum.

To be signed by the Seller and Listing Agent pertinent to the listing.

10. Modification to Listing Agreement (MLA - 3)
(property price change)

The sample (9A) used as is a price change form.

DO NOT change the price on Multiple Listing without the Sellers signature.

This is signed by the Seller and Listing Agent pertinent to the listing.

11. Seller / Borrower Non-Performance Addendum

This addendum used in this short sale must be approved by the Brokerage Firm / Broker.

The sample (12A) is a Listing Agreement Addendum.

This is when the seller does not comply to the agreements and documents signed to perform the Listing Agents fiduciaries duties.

To be signed Seller / Borrower.
(This must be completed in 7-14 days)

12. Arm's Length

Servicer / Lender / Investor may require all parties to sign an affidavit of "Arm's Length Transaction" No party to this contract is a family member, business associate, or share a business interest with the mortgagor. Further, there are no hidden terms or special understandings between the seller, buyer or their agents or mortgager. The Buyers and Sellers nor their agents have any agreements written or implicated that will allow the seller to remain in the property as renters or regain ownership of said property at any time after the execution of the short sale transaction. None of the parties shall receive any proceeds from this transaction except the sales commission. All parties are to sign buyers or sellers, buyer's agent and seller's agent.

13. Check List of 1-11 Seller / Borrower:

- 1) Financial Statements

- 2) Federal Tax Returns

- 3) Paycheck Stubs or Any Proof of Income

- 4) Bank Statements

- 5) Disclaimer: Seller / Borrower Listing Broker / Agent documentation

- 6) Hardship Letter from Seller / Borrower

- 7) Authorization to Release Information

- 8) Exclusive Right of Sale Listing Agreement

- 9) Comprehensive rider to the Residential Contract for sale and purchase (CR-1). G. Short Sale Approval Contingency.

- 10) Modification to Listing Agreement (Price Change)

- 11) Seller / Borrower Non-Performance Addendum

- 12) Arm's Length

- 13) Property Analysis Form

- 14) Photo Log

D) The First Document to Process

(Note) Number 1 the sample (6A) "Authorization To Release" form is in the Seller's Package.

Now is the time to hand the Authorization to Release over to your Coordinator / Processor if you have one.

(Note) Right to Financial Privacy Act (RFPA)

1) AUTHORIZATION TO RELEASE INFORMATION

Important document to start the process is the "Authorization to Release Information" for the following parties: Broker / Agent, Coordinator / Processor, Title Company and Attorney.

See the following example (6A) is the document that designed to be used for up to three Service / Lender / Investors. Add a fax cover sheet, see sample (23A).

This allows the Servicer / Lender / Investor to speak to you about the file.

WARNING: *This should be done within 24 hours of the Seller's / Borrower's listing appointment.*

Contact the Servicer / Lender / Investor using the phone number on the mortgage statement or other correspondence from the Servicer / Lender / Investor.

Inform the Servicer / Lender / Investor you have been authorized to discuss the file and that you have a Authorization To Release Information Form to send to them.

Ask them for the designated fax number and if anyone has been assigned to this file, if so, get there name and phone number.

The Servicer / Lender / Investor will inform you how long it will take to update the file with the Authorization to Release Information Form, normally 24 - 48 hours.

You will want to call back and make sure the file has been updated with the Authorization to Release Information Form (in three business days).

Ask again if anyone has been assigned to this file, if so get their name and phone number.

The representative of the Servicer / Lender / Investor may transfer you or give you a new contact number.

There are many scenarios that you should be aware:

1) They are referring you to the representative of the....

　A)　Short Sale Department

　B)　Loss Mitigation Department

　C)　Workout Department

　D)　Liquidation Department

　E)　Correspondence Department

The representative may inform you that the mortgage may have been assigned to a new Servicer / Lender / Investor and you may need to re-fax the Authorization To Release Information Form to a new number.

CHAPTER 11   Jump Start Your Wholesaling Business Now!

NOTES:

The Servicer / Lender / Investor is not be allowed by Law to speak to you without this Authorization to Release Information Form.

Without processing this Authorization in a timely manner, you will jeopardize your ability to negotiate with Servicer / Lender / Investor.

Upon successful transmission of the "Authorization" form. By showing the NFSSI logo on your fax cover letter, the Servicer / Lender / Investor will know that you understand the short sale process and that you have been certified.

2)   PRELIMINARY TITLE SEARCH

The following is critical to accelerate solving problems to the title, prior to closing (if applicable).

A preliminary title search should be done within 7 to 14 days so that you can verify the facts of the Seller / Borrower's listing appointments information. By acting on this you can identify any title problems to the short sale. This will allow you to expedite solutions to the title.

It is good to have a relationship with a Title Company / Attorney to facilitated title remedies.

3)   HOA FEES / PAYOFF LETTER

When there is a Homeowners Association, Condo Association, etc. the Title Company will need to get current Payoff and the Borrower needs to pay the fee for the Payoff Letter.

4) Arm's Length Transaction

Servicer / Lender / Investor may require all parties to sign an affidavit of "Arm's Length Transaction" No party to this contract is a family member, business associate, or share a business interest with the mortgagor. Further, there are no hidden terms or special understandings between the seller, buyer or their agents or mortgager. The Buyers and Sellers nor their agents have any agreements written or implicated that will allow the seller to remain in the property as renters or regain ownership of said property at any time after the execution of the short sale transaction. None of the parties shall receive any proceeds from this transaction except the sales commission. All parties are to sign buyers or sellers, buyer's agent and seller's agent.

Put The Ball In The Other Persons

E) Marketing your listing / Price Reduction

1) Within 24 to 48 hours in taking your listing you need to immediately enter the data into the Multiple Listing Service (MLS), as this is critical to your marketing strategy.

(See your MLS Rules and Regulations, and your Brokerage firm / Broker.)

The listing in the Multiple Listing Service (MLS) should disclose that the property is a short sale and must be a Service / Lender / Investor approved sale. This may be required by your local Multiple Listing Service (MLS). See your Brokerage Firm/Broker and Multiple Listing Service (MLS) for proper wording.

Also, in your Broker remarks you should disclose that "Commission is subject to Seller / Lender / Investor approval, with any reduction by Seller / Lender / Investor being shared between listing and Selling Broker on a 50 / 50 basis". See your Brokerage Firm / Broker or Multiple Listing Service (MLS) Rules and Regulations.

CHAPTER 11 Jump Start Your Wholesaling Business Now!

NOTES:

2) Additional website will allow for more exposure and opportunity for more showing appointments.

Example: www.wholesaleproperties.com specializing for Buyers and Sellers for short sale and real estate owned (REO) properties.

3) This MLS listing is critical to the Servicer / Lender / Investor as you have printed reports to verify the multiple listing history on the Seller / Borrower property.

4) This immediate marketing process will accelerate your listing to make your first price reduction as the Servicer / Lender / Investor will be considering a short sale.

5) The Servicer / Lender / Investor will see that the acceleration of this marketing for the Borrowers / Sellers property is

6) 40% of all sales transactions come from the property "FOR SALE" signs. The parties that are calling regarding the subject property may not be the interested property, but maybe interested in listing their property with you because of your visible sign in the neighborhood.

> *The rider (Price Reduction) sign on the property, brings additional attention to Buyers and shows that there is a motivated Seller.*

F) SETTING THE MARKET VALUE / PRICE REDUCTIONS

MODIFICATION TO LISTING AGREEMENT (MLA-3)
(property price change)

The sample (9A) is used for a price change.

DO NOT change the price of the Multiple Listing without the Sellers signature.

All signers on the Listing Agreement (7A) must sign.

ASSESSMENTS TO MAKE A MARKET VALUE AND PRICE REDUCTIONS

CHAPTER 11   Jump Start Your Wholesaling Business Now!

NOTES:

1) Current Active Inventory of Comparable Properties to the Subjects Property.

   Competitive Market Analyst (CMA)

   A) Short Sales

   B) Bank Owned Real Estate (REO)

   C) For Sale by Owner

   D) Standard Listing

   E) Excessive Inventory of Vacant Houses
   (Shadow Houses)

2) The sold in the last 30-60 days of the current inventory (CMA).

3) Condition of the Property, Cost of Repair / Inspection Report, see sample (14A)

4) Non-Conforming Use

   This applies to a property that is being used as a multi unit, but zoned for a single-family unit. This is an investors property; it needs to have a cash offer.

   The current lenders today do not do non-conforming loans, Therefore the demand for this type of property is limited to cash investors.

5) Consider the Foreclosure Timeline, if the Seller is in the foreclosure process.

CHAPTER 11   Jump Start Your Wholesaling Business Now!

NOTES:

HANDLING PRICE REDUCTION / TIME SENSITIVE

THE APPROACH

THE FACTORS ....

1)   No Showings   No Offers
   There is a problem with the listings.

2)   Showings   No Offers
   Listing price may be a factor.

3)   Showings   Low Ball Offers
   Price reduction may be your only option.

An additional suggestion to consider the following approach to price reductions. Consult your Brokers opinion on the market price. Get a second opinion.

From the time that you imputed your listing in the Multiple Listing Service (MLS), that starts the 15-day cycle.

Repeat the market value cycle every 15 days.

REPEAT THESE STEPS FOR PRICE REDUCTION

COMPETITIVE MARKET ANNALISIS (CMA)

This can be found in the Multiple Listing Service (MLS Exchange)

CHAPTER 11 Jump Start Your Wholesaling Business Now!

NOTES:

After logging into the MLS site:

1) Pull up the subject property

2) Click on the link that says "realist.com∆ (space that says tax)

3) Click on button that says "Comparable Properties"

4) Fill in property search options

5) Click on get Comparable

6) Pick out the best 3 properties that are the closest to the subject property.

7) Generate Comp Report

   The Seller must be motivated, as they are involved in the process. If the Seller is not going to commit to the price reductions, you must move on.

   The sample (12A) is a non-performance addendum.

   This addendum used in this short sale must be approved by the Brokerage Firm / Broker.

   This is when the Seller does not comply to the agreements and documents signed to perform the listing agents' fiduciaries duties.

"TIME IS AN ASSET"
   Mark Otis Cheeley

G)   Showing Appointments Log

The sample (SAL)

1) This is a log for the accountability for the listing agent of Buyers Agents setting up for the subjects property showings.

2) The log represents the interest or non-interest of the Seller / Borrower property.

3) The log represents a justification of the Price Reduction for the Seller / Borrower property as to the traffic for the Servicer / Lender / Invest.

4) When there is a Buyers offer, and the Seller accepts, this showing appointment log is optional for the Servicer / Lender / Investor to consider the offer.

The Brokerage Business / Broker may require your Broker / Agent Employment Agreement, that you must maintain showing logs.

H) Common Mistakes

1)   The short sale package must be complete before you send it to the Servicer / Lender / Investor.

Make sure that you send with your package all supporting documents to your Servicer / Lender / Investor

CHAPTER 11   Jump Start Your Wholesaling Business Now!

<u>AT THE SAME TIME.</u>

2) It is important that you make sure directly after your cover letter, to place the Preliminary Housing Urban Development Settlement Statement (HUD - 1).

3) Follow the instructions from the Service / Lender / Investor.

4) Make sure that your title search is complete when included in your package.

5) Do not send in an unrealistic offer to the Servicer / Lender / Investor.

6) When there are multiple loans you should negotiate with the second (and / or third if applicable) first.

   You need to do this so that you know what the second/third will accept as a payoff.

   This will help you negotiate with the 1st mortgage holder.

7) If there is an Equity Loan or a Home Equity Line Of Credit (HELOC) this will need to be negotiated also, before the 1st mortgage.

I) Non-controllable Issues

1) The Servicer / Lender / Investor sells the mortgage to another Servicer / Lender / Investor.

2) Seller / Borrower will not accept the offer.

3) Buyer's Agent does not send in a completed offer / package or sends in a package with missing support documents to the listing agent.

Example: The most updated Sale and Purchase contract, Short Sale Rider, Proof of Funds, Etc.

4) Seller / Borrower decides to do a Bankruptcy.

5) Servicer / Lender / Investor refuses to agree to your realistic offer.

J) The Lender / Investors Requirements for the Listing Agents Offer

The Lender / Investor conditions for the Listing Agent CAN NOT present an offer without a complete package.

The documents used in this offer have been approved by the Florida Association of Realtors® and the Florida Bar Association of Florida (FAR / BAR) use only.

For Legal Issues Contact the Florida Association of Realtors Legal Hot Line (407) 438-1409.

http://www.floridarealtor.org/member_signin.cfm?target=?LegalCenter/helpline/Member/Legal-Question-Form.cfm

For Use by The Members of the Florida Association of Realtors® Only

(Please have your Florida license number available when you call).

If any other state than Florida, you need to contact your States Association Board of Realtors® for your forms and documents.

CHAPTER 11   Jump Start Your Wholesaling Business Now!

NOTES:

(If you are a Licensed Salesperson with a Brokerage Firm/Broker typically they have their own approved required forms and documents. You must comply to your Broker requirements.)

The following documents are for a complete Buyer's Offer:

- 1. "As Is" Contract for Sale And Purchase - (ASSI-1) FAR/BAR

- 2. Comprehensive Rider to the Residential Contract for sale and Purchase, G. Short Sale approval contingency.

- 3. (FHA) Disclosure ≈Amendatory Clause / Real Estate Certification∆ (1 Page)

    This document is used when the Buyer has been approved for an (FHA) loan program.

- 4. Copy of the Deposit / Escrow Check

- 5. Escrow Deposit Receipt Verification (EDRV-1) FAR / BAR

- 6. Buyers Proof of Funds / Bank Statement
(Used for cash offer)

- 7. Financing, a Pre-qualifying letter from Buyer's Lender

- 8. Servicer / Lender / Investor may require all parties to sign an affidavit of "Arm's Length Transaction"

K) Sellers Multiple Offer and Acceptance

1) When the Listing Agent receives more than one offer on the Sellers property at the same time period.

2) When considering these offers you need to look at the details of the documents and make sure they are complete.

3) When you receive two offers and one is not a complete package that is not considered and offer.

4) On the package that is not complete you need to make a verbal call to the Selling Agent and notify him that he does not have the complete documents to pre- sent the offer and at that time you need to notify him that there is another offer and that package was complete. You can offer to email him or fax him the Lender / Investors requirements.

5) The Seller / Borrower accepted the first offer that was complete.

6) The Listing Agent needs to notify the second Buyers Agent that the Seller has accepted the first completed offer. (Professional courtesy)

If you are considering a backup offer see Comprehensive Rider to the Residential Contract for Sale and Purchase G. Short Sale Approval Contingency.

L) The Acceptance of Offer / Listing Status Change

1) When Seller and Buyer have an executed Contract, change the listing status in the Multiple Listing Service

(MLS) to Contingent. (MLS requires this under Rules and Regulations).

This stops the marketing process for the Buyer's Agent and stops showing appointments. Upon acceptance by the Service / Lender / Investor there will be conditions.

11.1 M) Submitting the Lender / Investor Package for Conditions and Approval

The authorization to release information should have been sent into the Servicer / Lender / Investor already, if not expedite immediately. (see section D-1 Authorization to Release Information) in this manual.

- 1. Fax Cover Sheet

- 2. Lender / Investor Cover Letter (Overview of Offer)

- 3. (HUD #1) Preliminary Settlement Statement
    This document is prepared by the Title Company from the contract, for the Lender / Investor to show their net proceeds from the sale.

- 4. "As Is" Contract for Sale and Purchase

- 5. Comprehensive Rider to the Residential Contract for Sale and Purchase G. Short Sale Approval Contingency.

- 6. (FHA) Disclosure - This document is used when the Buyer has approved for an (FHA) loan program.

- 7. Copy of the Deposit / Escrow Check

- 8. Proof of Funds - Bank Statement (When there is a cash offer from the Buyer)

- 9. Financing, a Pre-Qualifying letter from the Buyer's Lender

- 10. Authorization to Release Information

- 11. Hardship Letter handwritten by Seller / Borrower

- 12. Financial Statements

- 13. Paycheck Stubs or any proof of income (Copies of last 2 months)

- 14. Bank Statement, Seller / Borrower (Last 2 Months)

- 15. Federal Tax Return (Complete copies of last 2 years, or copy of extension)

- 16. Arm's Length

- 17. Exclusive Right of Sale Listing Agreement

- 18. Short Sale Addendum to Exclusive Right of Sale Listing Agreement

- 19. Cost of Repairs, Inspection Report (Photos of repairs needed)

- 20. Multiple Listing Service (MLS) The current listing of subject property.

- 21. Multiple Listing Service (MLS) Price History of the subject property.

- 22. Multiple Listing Service (MLS) Competitive Market Analysis (CMA)

CHAPTER 11   Jump Start Your Real Estate Business Now!

NOTES:

Contact the Servicer / Lender / Investor and ask them for the designated fax number to send in the fax package, and ask if anyone has been assigned to this file.

The Servicer / Lender / Investor will give you the fax number or email where to send the short sale package.

They are referring you to the representative of the ...

A) Short Sale Department

B) Loss Mitigation Department

C) Work Out Department

D) Liquidation Department

E) Correspondence Department

The representative may inform you that the mortgage may have been sold / assigned to a new Servicer / Investor and you may need to re-fax the Authorization To Release Information Form to a new number.

Add to the short sale package a fax cover sheet. Include the Borrower, Loan Number, Property Address and your name and contact information.

SHORT SALE PACKAGE.

Fax or Email your short sale package in for conditions and approval.

CHAPTER 11   Jump Start Your Wholesaling Business Now!

N) Maximizing your Income Stream / Commission

Listings are still the way to go, short sale listings will make you money. There is little if any competition for short sale listings.

It has never been so easy to get listings.

All you need is short sale knowledge to get the listings today.

The number of short sale closings are increasing. It is predicted in the year of 2019 that 85% of short sales will be closing.

The purpose of the Broker / Agent is to get the short sale listing and the purpose of the Coordinator / Processor is to close the short sale.

This allows the Broker / Agent to focus on what they do best, get more listings.

Brand yourself, market yourself in the short sale niche.

Dominate your local short sale market.

As a National Foreclosure Short Sales Institute "Certified Expert"^{SM} with our proven course you will increase your listings, closings and increase your income stream.

1) Two listings a week give you eight listings a month.

2) Closing 50% Equals = 4 closing sales (average sale $200,000)

CHAPTER 11 Jump Start Your Wholesaling Business Now!

3) 6% commission on an $200,000 sale with a split of 50/50 is $6,000 to the Listing Agent per transaction

4) At 4 closings with the average commission of $6,000 equals $24,000 for that month.

5) Paying a Coordinator / Processor 20% fee of the listing commission will give you $19,000 a month.

6) Having a Coordinator / Processor will give you more time to set new listing appointments.

7) Averaging 1 additional listing per week = 4 more per month.

8) 8 and 4 equals 12 (closing 50% of sales) = 6 sales @ average sale of $200,000 = $36,000 in closing commission.

9) Paying a Coordinator / Processor 20% fee of the listing commission will give you $28,800 a month.

10) Bonus: The National Association of Realtors survey says 40% of your leads that are calling from your sign are buyers.

11) Add to your income stream

12) Giving your short sale leads to a Buyer's Agent with a relationship of understanding that the commission split on the Buyers side will be 60/40.

13) At the rate of 40% your commission will increase on 6 sales equaling $14,400 in additional income.

14) 6 sales per month at $28,800 on the listing side, $14,400 on the buyers' side, equals $43,200.

Chapter 12

Problems to Avoid

PROBLEMS TO AVOID

1) The short sale package must be complete before you send it to the Servicer / Lender / Investor.

Make sure that you send with your package all supporting documents to your Servicer / Lender / Investor AT THE SAME TIME.

2) It is important that you make sure directly after your cover letter that place the Preliminary Housing Urban Development Settlement Statement (HUD - 1).

3) Follow the instructions from the Service / Lender / Investor.

4) Make sure that your title search is complete when included in your package.

5) Do not send in an unrealistic offer to the Servicer / Lender / Investor.

6) When there are multiple loans you should negotiate with the second (and / or third if applicable) first.

You need to do this so that you know what the second/third will accept as a payoff.

This will help you negotiate with the 1st mortgage holder.

7) If there is a Equity Loan or a Home Equity Line Of Credit (HELOC) this will need to be negotiated also, before the 1st mortgage.

Chapter 13

Non-Controllable Issues

NON-CONTROLLABLE ISSUES

1) The Servicer / Lender / Investor sells the mortgage to another Servicer / Lender / Investor.

2) Seller / Borrower will not accept the offer.

3) Buyer's Agent does not send in a completed offer / package or send in a package with missing support documents.

4) Seller / Borrower decides to do a Bankruptcy.

5) Servicer / Investor / Lender refuses to agree to your realistic offer.

Chapter 14

HUD - 1

HUD - 1 INSERT

U.S. Department of Housing and Urban Development Settlement Statement (HUD - 1)

These are the common lines that you should pay attention to:

101: Is the contract price from Buyer to the Seller?

201: Is the Deposit / Earnest money put down by the Borrower on the contract?

211: Are the County / Parish Taxes not paid? (this shows as a credit on the Buyers side).

503: Are there Existing Loan(s)? Often a ≈line of credit∆ that is to be paid off at the closing is placed here.

504: Payoff of first mortgage.

505: Payoff of second mortgage.

511: Are the County / Parish Taxes paid? (this shows as a payment on Seller's side)

700: Total Sales / Broker's Commission: This the commission.

1100 -1108: Title Charge: This section is about the fees from the title company and legal fees.

1200 -1205: Government Recording and Transfer Charges (City, County, State).

CHAPTER 14 HUD-1 Insert

NOTES:

1300 -1307: Additional Settlement Charges. Often these are blank / examples as follows:

1301: Survey

1302: Pest Inspections

1303: Shipping / Handling Fee

1304:

1305: Utilities

1306: Estimated Association Dues

1307: Estoppel Fee HOA

1400: Is the total settlement charges

Go to Front Page at the Bottom.

303: Cash from Buyer (This is the money that is owed from the Buyer)

603: Cash to Seller (This usually where the Seller is receiving monies from the sales)

Chapter 15

Frequently Asked Questions
What is a Short Sale?

FREQUENTLY ASKED QUESTIONS
WHAT IS A SHORT SALE?

In this changing housing market, the following questions and answers are intended to streamline your options.

What is a short sale?

A short sale is when a Servicer / Lender / Investor will take less than what is owed on the mortgage of the borrower.

Will this affect my credit rating?

Going through the foreclosure can knock 200 points off a FICO score, five times as much as the penalty for a short sale.

As the reporting of a short sale on their credit report drops 40 points average.

What is the advantage of a short sale?

In the event of a foreclosure a lender could seek a deficiency judgment in the amount that you owe. They could come after your personal assets and personal properties.

A foreclosure can impact your credit far more, especially in the long term. Some banks have been known not to report the short sale.

Your credit could recover from a short sale in less than 2 years, where as bankruptcy and foreclosure can take 7 to 10 years.

What is a deficiency judgment?

When the property sells for less than the mortgage owed, the amount is called a deficiency. The Lender / Investor has the right to collect the difference and pursue the collection with a deficiency judgment.

Example: The mortgage is $200,000 and Lender / Investor sells the property for $100,000 they could obtain a deficiency judgment for the $100,000.

(does not apply in California, Minnesota, Mississippi, Montana, North Dakota and West Virginia)

Can I stay in my house until the short sale is completed?

YES. You will not have to move out until the closing. In fact, if you are facing foreclosure and we are actively working with your bank, we can typically get your lender to delay the foreclosure proceedings and make it possible for you to stay in the home for some time.

Who Will Pay The Realtor® Commission And Clos-Ing Fees?

Your lender does. They pay a regular Real Estate Brokerage fee, just like a home seller would in a traditional transaction, and just like they would if they foreclosed on your home. Again, you pay $0 out of your pocket.

When can I buy a new home?

The Seller / Borrower has these options once your successful short sale has been completed.

CHAPTER 15 Frequently Asked Questions - What is a Short Sale

1) Thirty days from their successful short sale closing they are able to then purchase another new home, providing they have a credit score of 620 or above (as the reporting of a short sale on their credit report drops 40 points average).

2) One year if they have medical bills on their credit report.

3) Two years if they are applying for a Federal Housing Administration (FHA) loan.

4) Four years if they are applying for a conventional (CONV) Loan.

A Short Sale is Truly Your Best Option!

Will I get any financial Help for a Short Sale transaction?

On November 30, 2009 they passed the program of the Home Affordable Foreclosure Alternatives (HAFA) for qualified homeowners can get $3,000 dollars for relocation expenses.

The effective program date was April 5, 2010 the program will end on December 31, 2012.

Is a loan modification right for me?

If their Lender grants them a modification after many months of deliberating, they will take the amount they are behind and add it to the balance (This puts them further behind since they probably ALREADY owe more on the house than it is worth). If they are lucky, the Lender will drop the interest rates a couple of points. However, due to the amount the lender adds on to the balance, the savings will not be very significant.

A study from the Mortgage Bankers Association of modified loans showed that close to 90% of the homeowners were in foreclosure again within two years.

Can I do a short sale while I am in foreclosure and live in my primary home?

Yes. The lender / investor is happy to work with you on a short sale verses getting the property back from the sale at the courthouse steps. The foreclosure cost the lender / investor considerably more than a short sale.

The lender / investor like the idea that you are maintaining and keeping the property while the short sale transaction is to be completed, the lender / investor does not have to maintain the property or worry about vandalism.

If Seller / Borrower does nothing... The Lender will or has already filed foreclosure action against them, and eventually will attempt to sell their home at a sheriff sale, they will not receive anywhere close to what they owe on the property. The Lender / Investor may sue them and obtain a deficiency judgement for the difference between the total amount that was owed (including fees) and the amount they were able to sell it for. The Seller / Borrower will have a foreclosure on their credit report for 10 years or more and will not be able to buy another home with conventional financing for MANY, MANY years.

What happens to the money that is forgiven from my lender?

Any balance shortfalls on your mortgage(s) will likely be written off as a loss by your lender. Your lenders may also send you a "1099" for any balance forgiven.

Due to The Mortgage Debt Relief Act of 2007, you are NOT required to pay taxes on this money if you short sale your primary residence prior to 2012.

Is a Deed in Lieu right for me?

The bank still may have the right to pursue a deficiency judgment. If they have a second mortgage, they will most likely not agree unless the Seller / Borrower sign a promissory note for the balance. They still must pay the second mortgage!!! This will also have a very negative impact on their credit rating!

(Does not apply in California, Minnesota, Mississippi, Montana, North Dakota and West Virginia)

Do I give the listing to my Realtor that does not have Short Sale experience?

No! You need to get an experienced professional that has the qualifications of this transaction.

Your Realtor has to have your interest in mind for this transaction or the results could be disastrous!

A National Foreclosure Short Sale Institute ≈Certified Expert∆ᔆᴹ.

NFSSI provides a comprehensive Sellers Package to educate and facilitate a Win-Win results.

Only the best and the most experienced Realtor / Broker / Agents are in our team to facilitate your sale.

What would qualify me for a hardship?

Acceptable Hardships

- Death of Principal Borrower
- Death of Principal Borrower Family Member
- Serious illness of Principal Borrower
- Serious illness of Principal Borrower's Family Member
- Marital Problems (Divorce, Separation)
- Unemployment
- Lessened Income
- Property Abandonment
- Excessive Obligations
- Long Distance Employment Transfer
- Military Service
- Unable to Sell Property
- Unable to Rent Property
- Loss due to Accident, Fire or Natural causes
- Fraud
- Servicing Problems (ARM)
- Incarceration
- Payment Dispute
- Imposed Cost (Energy / Environment)
- Incurable Property Problems
- Ownership Transfer Pending
- Principle Borrower has Business Failure

Chapter 16

Title Frequently Asked Questions

TITLE FREQUENTLY ASKED QUESTIONS

What is a Title?

A Title is a legal document that is the foundation of property ownership. It is the owner's right to possess and use that property within certain limitations.

Why is transferring the Title to real estate different from transferring the Title to other items, such as a car? Because land is permanent and can have many owners over the years, various rights in land may have been acquired by others (such as mineral, air or utility rights) by the time you come into possession of it. So in order to transfer a clear title to a piece of land, it is first necessary to determine whether any rights are outstanding.

What is a Title search?

A Title search is a detailed examination of the historical records concerning a property. These records include deeds, court records, property and name indexes, and many other documents. The purpose of the search is to verify the seller's right to transfer ownership, and to discover any claims, defects, and other rights or burdens on the property.

What kinds of problems can a Title search reveal?

A Title search can show a number of title defects and liens, as well as other encumbrances and restrictions. Among these are unpaid taxes, unsatisfied mortgage, judgments against the owner and restrictions limiting the use of the land.

CHAPTER 16 Title Frequently Asked Questions

Are There Any Problems That A Title Search Can Not Reveal?

Yes. There are some "hidden hazards" that even the most diligent title search may never reveal. For instance, the previous owner could have incorrectly stated his marital status, resulting in a possible claim by his legal spouse. Other "hidden hazards" include things like fraud and forgery, defective deeds, mental incompetence, confusion due to similar or identical names and clerical errors in the records. These defects can arise after you've purchased your home and jeopardize your right to ownership.

What is Title Insurance?

Title insurance is your policy of protection against loss if any of these problems-even a ≈hidden hazard∆ results in a claim against your ownership.

How much could I lose if a claim is filed against my property?

That depends on the claim. In an extreme case, you could lose your entire home and property and still be liable to pay the balance of your mortgage. Most claims aren't that dramatic, but even the smallest claim can cost you money, time and aggravation, and you'll still have to pay costs for a legal defense.

How does Title Insurance protect my investment if a claim should arise?

If a claim is made against your property, Title Insurance will, in accordance with the terms of your policy, assure you of a legal defense and pay all court costs and related fees. Also, if the claim proves valid, you will be reimbursed for your actual loss up to the face amount of the policy.

The Owner Of The Property Has A Deed. Isn't That Proof Of Ownership?

Not necessarily. A deed is just a document by which the right of ownership in land is transferred, whatever that right may be. It's not proof of ownership, and it doesn't do away with rights that others may have in the property. In addition, a deed won't show you liens or claims that may be outstanding against the title.

Wouldn't an Abstract Show Property Limitations and Restrictions?

Maybe or maybe not. An Abstract is a history of the property title as revealed by the public records. Abstracts do not disclose "hidden hazards" and may contain errors.

What about an Attorney's opinion?

An Attorney's opinion is based on a search of the public records. So, once again, even the most exhaustive search of these records may not reveal everything. It's also important to remember that an attorney is not liable if you should suffer loss because of "hidden hazards" in the title.

The owner of the property I want to purchase has lived in the home for only 6 months. He had a title search done 6 months ago. Why do I need another one?

Because the owner could, in a very short time, do many things to encumber the Title. For example, he could grant easements or construct improvements which encroach on adjacent property. He could get married or divorced, or have a lien filed against the property. It is necessary to conduct an up-to-date Title search to uncover any such problems.

If the builder of my home already has title Insurance on the property, why do I need it again when I purchase the land from him?

A title policy insuring the builder does not protect you. Also, a great many things could have happened to the land since the builder's policy was issued. Liens, judgments and unpaid taxes for which prior owners were responsible may be disclosed after you purchase the property causing you aggravation and costing you money.

Are there different types of Title Insurance policies?

Yes. Basically, there are two different types of policies a lender's policy and an owner's policy. The lender's policy protects the lender's interest in the property as security for the outstanding balance under the buyer's mortgage. The owner's policy safeguards the buyer's investment or equity in the property up to the face amount of the policy. (Title insurers in many states offer increased policy cover- age through inflation endorsements to cover increases in value due to inflation.)

How much does Title Insurance cost?

Probably a lot less than you think. Charges vary in different sections of the country, but generally the cost of title insurance (including search, examination and related services) amounts to about one percent, or less, of the cost of the property. And unlike other insurance premiums which must be paid annually, a title insurance premium is paid one time only, usually at settlement.

How long does my coverage last?

For as long as you or your heirs retain an interest in the property.

Chapter 16 Title Frequently Asked Questions

Where can I get Title Insurance?

From any licensed Title Insurance Company or its representatives operating in your state. When choosing a title insurer, it is important that you look for a company with expertise and experience, as well as the financial strength to protect you should a claim arise. Your Broker or Attorney can recommend such a company.

Chapter 17

Web Links

WEB LINKS

Lenders

Realtors Association Florida Legal Hotline http://www.floridarealtors.org/member_signin.cfm?target=LegalCenter/helpline/Member/Legal-Question-Form.cfm

Mortgage Modification Resources

HUD - approved housing counselor 1-800-569-4287.

The Home Affordable Refinance Program
www.MakingHomeAffordable.gov

HOPE NOW
www.HopeNow.com

Homeowners Hope Hotline 1-888-995-HOPE.

Fannie Mae Loan Lookup
http://ww3.freddiemac.com/corporate

GMAC Homeowners Help Page
http://www.gmacmortgage.com/Resource_Center/homeowner_help/homeowner_help.html

GMAC Financial Analysis Form:
http://ww.gmacmortgage.com/pdfs/FinancialAnalysis.pdf

EQUATOR Agent Reference Guide for Bank of America Short Sales:
http://bankofamerica.reo.com/documents/AgentEducationGuide.pdf

Bank of America Homeowner Help
http://homeloanhelp.bankofamerica.com

Office of the Comptroller of the Currency
http://www.Helpwithmybank.gov

CHAPTER 17 Web Links

NOTES:

Lender / Investors

Hud Approved Counselors

Catholic Charities USA
www.catholiccharitiesusa.org

Citizen»s Housing and Planning Association, Inc.
www.chapa.org

Consumer Credit Counseling Service of Atlanta
www.cccsatl.org

HomeFree-USA
www.homefreeusa.org

Homeownership Preservation Foundation
www.995hope.org

The Housing Partnership Network
www.housingpartnership.net

Mission of Peace Housing Counseling Agency
www.missionofpeace.com

Mississippi Homebuyer Education Center
www.mhbec.com

The Mon Valley Initiative
www.monvalleyinitiative.com

Money Management International, Inc.
www.moneymanagement.org

National Council of La Raza
www.nclr.org

National Federation of Community Development Credit Unions
www.cdcu.coop

CHAPTER 17 Web Links

NOTES:

National Foundation for Credit Counseling
www.nfcc.org

The National Urban League
www.nul.org

Neighbor Works America
www.nw.org

Neighborhood Assistance Corporation of America (NACA)
www.naca.com

Rural Community Assistance Corp.
www.rcac.org

Structured Employment Economic Development Co.
www.seedco.org

Resources for Realtors
www.foreclosurelaws.org

www.realtytrac.com

www.mortgageloan.com/for-investors-four-tips-for-short-sale-purchase-1440

www.realtor.org

www.cbsnews.com/stories/2007/06/21/earlyshow/contibutors/raymrtin/main2961274.shtml

http://www.realtytimes.com/rtpges/20070409_shortsale.htm

FreddieMac: Advoiding Foreclosure and Beware of Scam Artist

www.freddiemac.com/avoidforclosure

www.freddiemac.com/corporate/buyown/english/owning/avoid_foreclosure.html

CHAPTER 17 Web Links

NOTES:

HUD: Tips for Avoiding Foreclosure
www.hud.gov/foreclosure.index.cfm

The Federal Trade Commission: Mortgage Payments Sending You Reeling? Here's what to do.
www.ftc.gov/bcp/edu.pubs.consumer/homes/rea04.shtm

National Consumer Law Center: Tips for Consumers on Avoiding Foreclosure Rescue Scams
www.mass.gov/eoca/docs/dob.avoidscam.pdf

NeighborWorks Center for Foreclosure Solutions
www.nw.org/network.neighborworksProgs/foreclosuresolutions/default.asp

Customizable flyer to Avoid Foreclosure
www.efanniemae.com/sf/homestay/doc/avoid/foreclosurefactsheet.doc

Mortgage Bankers Association foreclosure statistics
www.mortgagebankers.org/NewsandMedia/PressCenters.58758.htm

Credit Score information:
www.myfico.com/CreditEducation/whatsInYourScore.aspx

www.votesmartflorida.org/mx/hn.asp?id=VoterGuide_jan08_Amendment1

www.floridataxwatch.org/resources/pdf/WhattheOct2007SpeciaSessionDoftheLegisIaturedid.pdf

www.yeson1florida.com/resources/downloads/yeson1_comparison_chart.pdf

FHA Secure
www.hud.gov/news/fhahandout.pdfportal.hud.gov/fha/rreference/m12007/0711mil.doc

Mortgage Forgiveness Debt Relief Act of 2007
www.govtrck.us/congress.bill.xpd?bill=h110-3648

Chapter 18

Short Sale Definitions

SHORT SALE DEFINITIONS

Authorization Letter: This gives the Servicer / Lender / Investor permission by the Seller / Borrower to speak with the Broker / Agent, Coordinator / Processor, Attorney and Title Company.

Brokers Price Opinion: A value of a subject property for the Servicer / Lender / Investor done by a third party real estate Broker / Agent.

Coordinator / Processor: A seasoned professional that puts the short sale package in order for the Servicer / Lender / Investor, sends in the short sale package and keeps track of it by calling the Servicer / Lender / Investor.

Default: Is when the borrower has stopped making their mortgage payments, the Service / Lender / Investor has the right to enforce legal proceedings.

Deficiency Judgement: When the property sells for less then the mortgage is owed, amount is called a deficiency. The Lender / Investor has the right to collect for the difference and purse the collection with a court ordered deficiency judgment.

Deed In Lieu: The Seller / Borrower signs the deed back over to the Lender / Investor instead of the property going through the foreclosure process.

Distressed Property: Property that is under a foreclosure order or is advertised for sale by its mortgagee. Distressed property usually fetches a price that is below its market value.

Forbearance: When the Lender / Investor agrees not to foreclose in the exchange for a repayment plan by the borrower.

CHAPTER 18 Short Sale Definitions

Foreclosure: A legal process by which the Servicer / Lender / Investor or other lien holders obtain a court order to repossess and sell the real property and keep the proceeds to pay off its mortgage and any legal cost.

This process is done when the borrower is in default by not paying the mortgage payment.

Hardship Letter: Usually a handwritten letter by the Seller / Borrower to the Servicer / Lender / Investor explaining the reason(s) they are unable to make or keep making the mortgage payments.

Lis Pendens: Is pending litigation, a filed document at the records office in the county where the property is located. This is the beginning of the foreclosure process.

Loss Mitigator: Works with the Servicer / Lender / Investor, who negotiates the short sale package.

Notice of Sale: Public filings, recordings, posting, notifications, and advertisements that are required by law, public

Pre-Foreclosure: The Servicer / Lender / Investor has filed notice with the court, first stage of the foreclosure process.

Preliminary HUD - 1: Settlement Statement where the seller and buyer and subject property address information is in one place, shows where all the monies and to whom, shows the Servicer / Lender / Investor their estimated net proceeds.

REO Real Estate Owned: REOs are what the Banks / Lenders / Investors call their inventory of real estate property that they have taken back by the foreclosure process.

Short Pay: When the lender / Investor sells the Mortgage back to the Seller / Borrower for a one-time cash payoff, usually less than is owed.

CHAPTER 18 Short Sale Definitions

NOTES:

Short Sale: The Lender / Investor will take less then what is owed on the mortgage.

Underwater: When the borrowers' homes are worth less then the mortgage.

Chapter 19

General Glossary Real Estate Terms

CHAPTER 19 General Glossary Real Estate Terms

GLOSSARY

Abandonment:	A surrender of rights; point when a broker makes no effort to service or sell listed property; failure to perform.
A Bar Sale:	Memory aid for the eight major services of real estate.
Absentee Owner:	A property holder who does not reside on the property and who usually relies on a property manager to supervise the investment.
Abstract of Title:	Condensed history of title to real property consisting of a summary of the links in the "chain of title" extracted from documents bearing on the title status.
	Acceleration Clause: Stipulation in a mortgage that the entire unpaid balance of the debt may become due and payable if a default of expressed conditions should occur.
Acceptance:	Voluntary receipt of an item offered by another.
Accounts Payable:	Money owed by a business (liabilities.)
Accounts Receivable:	Money owed to a business (assets).
Accretion:	Gradual addition of land caused by natural forces, such as wind, tide, flood or watercourse deposits.
Accrued Interest:	Interest which has been earned by a lender, but which has been allowed to accumulate and will be paid by the borrower at a later date.
Acknowledgment:	Certification of a document by a notary public; formal declaration of an act before a competent official.
Acquisition:	The act or process by which a person acquired ownership of property.
Acre:	A measure of land equaling 160 square rods, or 4,840 square yards, or 43,560 square feet.
Actual Notice:	Informing any interested party of a right, title or interest in property by possession of the property.
Adjudication	A judicial or court decision.
AGI:	Adjustable Gross Income. Total income received from income property.
ARM:	Adjustable-Rate Mortgage. A financing technique in which the lender can raise or lower the interest rate according to a set index.
Ad Valorem:	According to the value; in proportion to worth.
Advance Fee:	Collection of a fee prior to a transaction actually closing or prior to the performance of a service.
Adversary Opponent:	A person or group that opposes one another.
Adverse Interest:	A purpose in opposition to the interest of another party (as, for example, with a buyer and a seller).
Adverse possession:	A method of obtaining title to real property by occupying it in an open and hostile manner contrary to the interests of the owner.
Affidavit:	A sworn statement written down before a notary or public official.

CHAPTER 19 General Glossary Real Estate Terms

NOTES:

After-Tax Cash Flow:	(See Contract for deed.)
Agency:	Express or implied authorization for one person to act for another; one of the divisions of the real estate business.
Agent:	A representative; one who is authorized to act on behalf of another.
Agreement for Deed:	(See Contract for deed.)
Air Rights:	The freedom to use the open space above a property.
Alienation:	The act of transferring ownership, title or an interest or estate in real property.
Allodial System:	A theory of land ownership that individuals may own land free of the rights of an overlord.
Alluvion:	The increase of land by the gradual and imperceptible action of natural forces (e.g., alluvial deposits of sand and mud on a riverbank).
A.L.T.A.	A form of title insurance policy issued by a title insurance company, who will expand the risks normally. Insurance policy must be renewed to continue in effect.
Amortization:	Payment of a debt by regular installment payments.
Annual Debt Service:	The amount of money required each year for the payment of all mortgage interest and principal.
APR:	Annual Percentage Rate. Total yearly cost of credit.
Annuity:	A series of equal payments to be made over a period of time, or a lump sum to be made in the future.
Appeal:	A request to some authority for a decision or judgment.
Applicant:	A person who applies for something; a candidate.
Appraisal:	Professional service provided by a registered, licensed or certified appraiser and provides an estimate of value. Appraisers render a "professional" serve.
Appreciation:	An increase in value.
Arbitration:	The act of having a third party settle a dispute between two parties.
Arrears:	The state of being behind in the discharge of an obligation; paid at the end of the period for which due (the opposite of in advance).
Assessed Value:	Worth established for each unit of real property for tax purposes by a county property appraiser.
Assessment:	The imposition of a tax or charge according to a preset rate; the allocation of the proportionate individual share of a common expense in a condo or co-op building.
Asset:	Anything of value.
Assignee:	Person to whom a right or interest is transferred.
Assignment:	Written instrument that serves to transfer the rights or interests of one person to another.
Assignor:	Person who gives his or her legal rights or interests to another person.
Associate:	Person working for a broker.

CHAPTER 19 General Glossary Real Estate Terms

Association:	An organization of persons having a common interest (e.g., condominium association, homeowner's association).
Assumption Fee:	A charge made by a lender for changing over and processing new records for a new owner who is assuming an existing loan.
Assumption of Mortgage:	The taking over of an existing mortgage by a buyer.
Attachment:	A legal writ obtained to prevent removal of property that is expected to be used to satisfy a judgment.
Attorney-in-fact:	One who is authorized to perform certain acts for another under a power of attorney.
Attorney, Power of:	POA. Designation of another person to act for a principal who may not be present.
Balance Sheet:	A financial document used to show the assets, liabilities, and net worth of a business at a specific time.
Balloon Mortgage:	A financing device requiring periodic payments of a smaller amount that is necessary to fully amortize the principal borrowed. A single, large (balloon) payment at maturity is required to pay off the debt in full. Balloon payment the final installment payment on a note that is greater than the preceding installment payments and pays the note off in full.
Bank:	A financial institution that rents money from others and guarantees the return of that money. It, in return, lends the money out and takes the risk of any loss.
Bankruptcy:	A court action declaring a person free of most debt, due to the inability of the person to pay.
Bargain & Sale Deed:	A type of deed in which title is transferred and a limited number of warranties are made respecting title to or use of the property.
Base Line:	An imaginary line running east and west and crossing a principal meridian at a definite point; used by surveyors for reference in locating and describing land under the government survey system.
Basic/Primary Industry:	A business that attracts outside money into the area.
Before-Tax Cash Flow:	(*See* Cash throw off.) Biennium (Biennial) A period of two years.
Bilateral Contract:	An agreement wherein both parties are legally obligated to each other to perform.
Binder:	A memorandum given subject to the writing of a formal contract for sale, usually acknowledging receipt of a portion of the down payment for purchase of real property.
Blanket Mortgage:	One mortgage covering two or more parcels.
Blind Ad:	An advertisement of a principal's property providing only a telephone number, a post office box and/or address without the licensed name of the brokerage firm. Blockbusting The illegal practice of inducing homeowners to sell their property by making misrepresentations regarding the entry or prospective entry of minority persons in order to cause a turnover of properties in the neighborhood; discriminatory acts against sellers.

CHAPTER 19 General Glossary Real Estate Terms

Blockbusting:	The illegal practice of inducing homeowners to sell their property by making misrepresentations regarding he entry or prospective entry of minority persons in order to cause a turnover of properties in the neighborhood; discriminatory acts against sellers.
Bona-fide:	Without deceit or fraud; genuine; in good faith. Borrower (debtor) the mortgagor; one who gives a mortgage as security for a debt.
Borrower:	(debtor) The mortgagor; Individual or institution receiving funds in the form of a loan and obligated to repay the loan, usually with interest.
Branch Office:	A business location other than the real estate broker's principal place of business.
Breach:	Failure to do or perform what has been promised. Bridge Loan A short term loan that bridges a gap between two other loans, usually intended to provide temporary financing in a period between two basically different loan types.
Bridge Loan:	A short term loan that bridges a gap between two other loans, usually intended to provide temporary financing in a period between two basically different loan types.
Broker:	Generally, a special agent who acts as an intermediary between two parties and negotiates contracts between them.
Brokerage:	A broker's commission.
Broker-Salesperson:	An individual who is qualified to be issued a broker's license but who operates as a salesperson in the employ another.
Building Code:	A government ordinance regulating construction practices and materials.
Bullet Loan:	A mortgage loan with no amortization (usually five years in term), payable at interest-only payments.
Bulk Sale:	Any transfer of the major part of the assets of a business (e.g., materials, inventory, real property); not a transfer in the ordinary course of business.
Business Brokerage:	The sale, purchase or lease of businesses that provide goods and/or services.
Business Trust:	(syndicate) a group of people who associate with each other for the purpose of purchasing shares or units at a specified amount per unit, with the money raised to be used to purchase the real property, often for subdividing and resale.
Buy Down:	A financing technique in which points are paid to the lender by the seller or builder that lowers (buys down) the effective interest rate paid by the buyer/borrower, thus reducing the amount of the monthly payment for a set period of time.

CHAPTER 19 General Glossary Real Estate Terms

Buyer's Market:	The supply of available properties exceeds the demand.
Capital:	The collective wealth (money and property) of a person or business; the investment in a property. (*See also* Equity.)
Capital Asset:	Certain property held by a taxpayer, not including inventory for sale to customers.
Capital-Deficit Area:	A region where the total amount of local savings (investment capital) is not sufficient to finance economic development already under way in that area.
Capital Gain:	The profit from the sale of a capital asset, including real property.
Capitalization Rate:	The relationship between the net income from a real estate investment and the present value.
Cash-Breakeven-Ratio:	The relationship of all cash charges to potential gross income.
Cash Flow:	(after-tax cash flow) The spendable income from an investment after deducting all operating and fixed expenses.
Cash-On Cash Return:	(*See* Equity dividend rate.)
Cash Throw-Off:	(before-tax cash flow; gross spendable income) The resulting amount when annual debt service is subtracted from net operating income. Caveat emptor Let the buyer beware!
C, C, & R:	Covenants, Conditions, and Restrictions affecting the use of a property.
Cease & Desist Order:	An action by a government agency to require a person or business to stop an illegal or unfair practice.
Censure:	An official act of strong disapproval.
Certificate Of Title Opinion:	(opinion of title) A document signed by a title examiner (attorney or title company agent) stating the judgment that, based on an examination of the public records, the seller has good title to the property being conveyed to the buyer (not to be confused with title insurance).
Certified Appraiser:	(*See* State-certified appraiser.)
Certiorari, Writ Of:	An order to bring from a lower court to an appellate court an action or record of proceedings in a case.
Chain of Title:	A successive listing of all previous holders of title (owners) back to an acceptable starting point.
Chattel:	Any item of personal property (*see also* Personal property).
Check:	A square measuring 24 miles on each side and representing the largest unit of measure in the government survey system.
Citation:	A statement of an alleged violation and the penalty to be imposed.
Clause:	A distinct provision in a written document.
Client:	A person or firm who receives professional services from a broker.

CHAPTER 19 General Glossary Real Estate Terms

Closing:	Final settlement between the buyer and seller; the date on which title passes from the seller to the buyer.
Closing Costs:	Fees and expenses paid by the borrower at closing.
Cloud on Title:	Any defect, valid claim or encumbrance that serves to impair the title or curtail an owner's rights.
Co-Broker:	A person who finds prospects for the broker and receives a finder's fee for his information.
Collateral:	Real or personal property pledged as security on a debt.
Collateral loans:	Mostly made available to persons or companies with sufficient collateral.
Collusion:	Two or more parties jointly attempting to defraud a third party.
Color of Title:	A condition in which ownership of real property appears to be good but is not good because of a defect.
Commingle:	(intermingle) To mix together money or a deposit with personal funds; combine.
Commission:	Compensation paid to a broker or salesperson for successfully concluding a real estate transaction; short form for Florida Real Estate Commission (FREC).
Commitment:	A firm agreement made by a lender to provide funds for the borrower at a specified future date. The commitment documents stipulate amount and terms of the promised loan.
Common Elements:	The parts of a multiple-ownership property not included in the units; those parts in which each unit owner holds in undivided interest.
Common Law:	A system of law based on accepted customs and traditions.
Community Property:	Real property acquired during a marriage.
Comparable sales approach:	A method for estimating the market value of a property by comparing similar properties to the subject property.
Comparative market analysis	(See comparable sales approach).
Complainant:	A person who makes an allegation or a charge against another (the respondent).
Compound Interest:	Interest paid on original principal and on the accrued and unpaid interest which as accumulated.
Complaint	Formal allegation or charge.
Comprehensive Plan:	(master plan) A statement of policies for the future physical development of an area (e.g., city, county, region).
Concealment:	The act of keeping from sight or keeping secret.
Condemnation:	The taking of private real property for a public purpose under the right of eminent domain for a fair price.
Condominium:	A multi-unit project consisting of individual ownership of a dwelling unit and undivided ownership of common areas.
Consideration:	Inducement offered to conclude a contract.
Consolidation Loan:	A loan made to combine several smaller loans, usually to reduce the amount of payments made each month, or to get a lower interest rate.

CHAPTER 19 General Glossary Real Estate Terms

Construction Loan: A loan made for the construction of commercial or residential buildings. funds are usually disbursed to the contractor/builder during construction.

Construction Loan w/Takeout: A construction loan made after a sale of property or long-term financing has been contracted. Thereby the construction lender has a guaranteed source of funds upon completion of construction.

Constructive Notice: The recording of a document or an instrument in the public records designed to give adequate notice to all.

Consumer Price Index: (CPI) A measurement of average price changes of goods and services using a base period.

Contract: An agreement between two or more competent parties to do, or not do, some legal act for a legal consideration.

Contract for deed A financing technique wherein the seller agrees to deliver the deed at some future date and the buyer takes possession while paying the agreed amount (also called a "land contract", an "installment sales contract" and an "agreement for deed").

Conventional Mortgage: A real estate loan granted that is neither FHA-insured nor VA-guaranteed.

Conversion: Unauthorized use or retention of money or property that rightfully belongs to another person.

Convertible Mortgage: A financing instrument allowing a change from an adjustable-rate to a fixed-rate mortgage.

Conveyance: Written instrument that serves to transfer an interest in real property from one party to another.

Cooperative: A multi-unit project consisting of individual dwelling units owned by the corporation in which the individual apartment tenants' own stock rather than owning their respective units.

Co-ownership: (concurrent or multiple ownership) title to real property held by two or more persons at the same time.

Corporation: An artificial or fictitious person formed to conduct specified types of business activities.

Corporation-Not-For-Profit: An artificial or fictitious person organized for business purposes and similar to a corporation for profit.

Corporation Sole: An artificial or fictitious person formed by an ecclesiastical body.

Cost: The amount to produce or acquire something.

Cost-depreciation approach: A method for estimating the market value of a property based on the cost to buy the site and to construct a new building on the site, less depreciation.

Counseling: One of the component activities of the agency division of the real estate business.

Counteroffer: A rejection of the original offer by proposing a new offer, thereby terminating the original offer.

Covenant: A warranty, guarantee or promise formally given in a legal document.

CHAPTER 19 General Glossary Real Estate Terms

Credit:	As a verb, to make an entry on the right or credit side of an account; as a noun, payment or value received.
Credit Application:	A form filled out by the borrower who is trying to establish credit, with information about his income, residence and existing debt.
Credit Bureau:	An agency which assembles credit information on consumer which they supply to others so that the credit standing, and capacity of the consumer can be established.
Credit Lease Loan:	Financing based on credit of lessee instead of the value of his property.
Creditor:	A lender; person or business entity to whom a debt is owed.
Credit Rating:	An evaluation of a person's or firm's previous credit experience.
Culpable Negligence:	Inadequate attention to duties and obligations by one who knows, or should know, what is required of him or her.
Curbstone Operation:	Conducting business without maintaining an office.
Current Asset:	Any asset that can be converted into cash on a short notice (stocks or bonds).
Customer:	One with whom the broker or salesperson hopes to be successful in accomplishing the purpose of employment; a prospect.
Damages:	Losses incurred as a result of a breach of contract or some other cause (see also Liquidated and Unliquidated damages).
Debit:	As a verb, to make an entry on the left or charge side of an account; as a noun, a charge or expense.
Debt-Service Coverage Ratio:	The relationship of net operating income to the mortgage payment.
Decedent:	A deceased person, usually one who has recently died.
Declaration of Trust:	A formal instrument filed by a business trust with the department of State as a prerequisite for creation the trust.
Declaratory Judgment:	A course of action declaring rights claimed under a contract or statue intended to prevent loss or to guide performance by the party or parties affected.
Declining Balance:	The remaining balance of a debt following a monthly payment.
Dedicated Land:	An offer of land for some public use, by an owner, together with acceptance by or on behalf of the public.
Deed:	A type of conveyance; a written instrument to transfer title to real property from one party to another.
Default:	Failure to comply with the terms of an agreement or to meet an obligation when due.

CHAPTER 19 General Glossary Real Estate Terms

Defeasance Clause: A provision in a mortgage that specifies the terms and conditions to be met in order to avoid default and thereby defeat the mortgage.

Defect (See Cloud on title.)

Defer: To postpone payment.

Defendant: The person or party being sued or charged.

Deficiency Decree: Judgment brought when a mortgage is foreclosed and the sale proceeds fail to offer the costs of the sale, taxes and the unpaid mortgage balance.

DHUD: Department of Housing and Urban Development

Delinquent: Payment which is overdue.

Demand: (principle of supply and demand) The quantity of goods or services wanted by consumers.

Demand Deposit: A checking account; payable on demand by holder.

Denial: A refusal or rejection.

Density: The number of homes or lots per acre.

Deposit: Earnest money or some other valuable consideration given as evidence of good faith to accompany an offer to purchase or rent (see also Binder and Earnest money).

Deposition: Written testimony of a witness under oath.

Depreciation: A loss in value for any reason; a deduction for tax purposes.

Descent: The passage of title to real property upon the death of the owner to his or her legal descendants.

Development Of Regional Impact (DRI): A large project affecting more than one county.

Devise: A gift of real property by a will.

Devisee: One who receives real property under a will.

Devisor: One who gives real property through a will.

Direct Participation Program (DPP): An investment entity managed by a third party for the investors who share in the profit and loss of the investment (e.g., real estate, oil and gas).

Discounting: A method for increasing a lender's yield; a practice that allows VA mortgages to be competitive with FHA and conventional mortgages (see also Point, mortgage discount).

Disintermediation: A disengagement process when depositors withdraw money from savings for direct investment in stocks, money market funds and other securities.

Documentary Stamp Tax On Deeds: State tax required on all deeds or other documents used as conveyances. The charge is based on the total purchase price.

Documentary Stamp Tax On Notes: State tax required on all promissory notes. The cost is based on the face value of the note.

CHAPTER 19 General Glossary Real Estate Terms

Down payment:	A portion of a purchase price paid prior to closing the transaction. Earnest money may be part of or the entire down payment.
Draw (installment):	Disbursement made by a lender to a builder.
Dual Agency:	Representing both principals in a transaction.
Due-on-Sale Clause:	A provision in a conventional mortgage that entitles the lender to require the entire loan balance to be paid in full if the property is sold.
Earnest Money:	A sum that, if a contract is executed, is applied against the down payment (see also Binder and Deposit).
Easement:	A right, privilege or interest in real property that one individual has in lands belonging to another; a legal right to trespass; right-of-way authorizing access to or over land.
Economic life:	The period of time a property may be expected to be profitable or productive; useful life.
Effect a Sale:	A provision in a listing contract requiring the broker to obtain a signed contract from a ready, willing, and able buyer on the terms specified.
Effective Gross Income (EGI):	The resulting amount when vacancy and collection losses are subtracted from potential gross income.
Elective Share:	An estate defined as consisting of 30 percent of the decedent's personal property and Florida real property, except homestead-exempt property and claims.
Eminent Domain:	The constitutional right given to a unit of government to take private property involuntarily if taken for public use and a fair price is paid to the owner.
Employer:	The individual who hires the services of another.
Empty-nester:	Older parents whose housing needs change after their children have moved away.
Encroachment:	Unauthorized use of another person's property.
Encumbrance:	Any lien, claim or liability affecting the title or attaching to real property.
Encumbrance Clause:	A provision in a deed to real proper- ty that warrants that no liens, claim or liabilities exist on the property being conveyed, except as specified.
End Loan:	A property construction loan; loan on an individual condo unit.
Equitable Title:	The right of a vendee to obtain absolute ownership of property to which the vendor has legal title; the interest held by a vendee under a sales contract or contract for deed; beneficial interest.
Equity:	The market value of a property less any debt against it; in a business entity, assets minus liabilities equals capital (owner's equity); a system of legal rules administered by a court of chancery.

CHAPTER 19 General Glossary Real Estate Terms

NOTES:

Equity Dividend Rate: (cash-on-cash return) The relationship of annual cash throw-off to original equity investment.

Equity of Redemption: The right of a mortgagor, before a foreclosure sale, to reclaim forfeited property by paying the entire indebtedness.

Escalator Clause: A provision in a mortgage permitting the lender to increase or decrease the interest rate that is usually tied to an event or a contingency.

Erosion: Gradual loss of land due to water or other natural causes.

Escalator Clause: A provision in a mortgage permitting the lender to increase or decrease the interest rate that is usually tied to an event or a contingency.

Escheat: Reversion of property to the state when an owner dies without leaving a will or any known heirs.

Escrow Account: (trust account) An account in a bank, title company, credit union, savings and loan or trust company used solely for safekeeping customer funds and not for deposit of personal funds; impound account.

Escrow Disbursement Order (EDO): A course of action for determining the disposition of a contested deposit.

Estate Tenancy: The interest one holds in real property; the total of one's property and possessions.

Estate by The Entireties: A tenancy created by husband and wife jointly owning real property with instant and complete right of survivorship.

Estate for life: (See Life estate.)

Estate for Years: A tenancy measured from a starting date to a termination date (may be for a few days or longer than any natural life; e.g., a leasehold is an estate for years).

Estate in Fee: (See Fee simple estate.)

Estate in Reversion: An estate that comes back to the original estate.

Estate in Sole: Real property owned by a corporation sole. Estate of freehold (See Freehold estate.)

Estate of Remainder: An estate that can become effective only after another estate has terminated.

Estoppel A Principle of law that prohibits (stops) a person from defending him or herself against his or her own acts or lack of action.

Estoppel Certificate: A written statement that bars the signer from making a claim inconsistent with the instrument (commonly used with a mortgage assumption).

ET AL: And others.

ET UX: And wife.

Ethics: The moral obligations and duties that remember of a profession or craft owes to the public, to a client or to other members of the profession or craft.

Evict: A legal method to remove tenants from a property. Evidence Any profit that may legally be admitted in settlement of an issue.

Exclusion: The right of an owner to control entry onto the

Federal National Mortgage Association (FNMA) ("Fannie Mae"): A private institution in the secondary mortgage market that buys and sells mortgages.

Federal Reserve System (the Fed): A central banking authority that influences the cost, availability and supply of money.

Federal Trade Commission (FTC): A federal agency that investigates and eliminates unfair and deceptive trade practices.

Fee Simple Estate: The most comprehensive and complete interest one can hold in real property; freehold estate.

Fictitious Name: (See Trade name.)

Fiduciary: A person in a position of trust and confidence with respect to another person.

Fiduciary Relationship: An alliance of trust and confidence that creates a moral and legal obligation when extended by one person and accepted by another.

Final Order: A decision rendered by FREC.

Find A Purchaser: A provision in a listing contract requiring a broker to produce a ready, willing and able buyer or offer on the terms specified.

Financial Analysis: Investor's determination of the value of a property according to his or her specific needs.

Financial Leverage: The use of other peoples' money for investment purposes.

Finder's Fee: The fee paid to someone not requiring a license for information helpful to a broker.

First Deed of Trust: A deed of trust recorded first, equivalent to a first mortgage.

First Mortgage: The first recorded mortgage on a property. Fixture An object that was once considered to be person- al property but has become real property because of attachment to, or use in, an improvement to real property. Flexible seller A seller who is willing to sell property in anon- traditional manner. This person may be flexible in terms, price, or both.

Follow-up: What a salesperson does after a sale to maintain customer contact and goodwill.

Forbearance: Act by which a creditor extends time for payment.

Forced Sale: The sale of a property used as security for a loan in order to repay creditor(s) in the event of a default on the loan.

Foreclosure: A court process to transfer title to real proper- ty used as security for debt as a means of paying the debt by involuntary sale of the property.

Formal Contract: Any agreement that contains all the essentials of a contract, including that it is in writing and under seal.

CHAPTER 19 General Glossary Real Estate Terms

Formal Hearing: (See Hearing.)

Fraud: The intent to misrepresent a material fact or to deceive to gain an unfair advantage or to harm another person.

Free and Clear: Title to real property that is absolute and unencumbered.

Free Dealership: Right given to a woman in some states to purchases or convey real estate, sue or be sued in her name without the joinder of her husband.

Freehold Estate: A tenancy in real property with no set termination date that can be measured by the lifetime of an individual or can be inherited by heirs.

Further Assurance: A provision in a deed containing a covenant or warranty to perform any further acts the grantee (buyer) might require to perfect title to the property. General lien A claim that may affect all of the properties of a debtor.

Going Concern: Value The worth of a business, including real estate, goodwill and earning capacity.

Goodwill: An intangible asset (value) of a business. Government land survey system (rectangular method) A type of land description, developed by the federal government for subdividing lands utilizing surveying lines.

Government Lot: Fractional piece of land less than a quarter section resulting from geographical features (e. g., lakes, streams) interfering with land surveying.

Government National Mortgage Association (GNMA) ("Ginnie Mae"): A federal agency designed to handle special-assistance functions for certain loans and securities Grantee Party who receives a deed or grant; buyer. Granting clause (premises clause) the provision in a deed that specifies the names of the parties involved, the words of conveyance and a description of the property.

Grantor: Party who signs and gives a deed; seller.

Green Belt Law: Florida legislation that authorizes county property appraisers to assess land used for agricultural purposes according to its current value as agricultural land.

Gross Income Multiplier (GIM): A rule of thumb for estimating the market value of commercial and industrial proper- ties; the ratio to convert annual income into market value. Gross rent multiplier (GRM) A rule of thumb for estimating the market value of income producing residential proper- ty; the ratio to convert rental income into market value.

Group license: A right granted a salesperson or broker-salesperson to work various properties owned by affiliated entities under one individual or group (his or her employing broker).

Ground Lease: An agreement made for the use of the land only.

Habendum Clause: A provision in a deed to real property that stipulates the estate or interest the grantee is to receive and the type of title conveyed.

CHAPTER 19 General Glossary Real Estate Terms

Handbook:	Published by the Florida Real Estate Commission for study and guidance of students, applications, licensees and member of the general public on Florida. Statute 475 and other laws, acts, rules and regulations.
Hazard Insurance:	Coverage by contract whereby one party undertakes to guarantee another party against loss resulting from physical damage to real property.
Hearing:	A session in which testimony and arguments are presented, especially before an official.
Hearing Officer:	An attorney employed by the Division of Administrative Hearings Department of Administration, to hear complaints and issue recommended order.
Highest And Best Use:	A principle of value that focuses on the most profitable, legal use to which a property can be put. Homestead Term used to describe three separate but related situations: (1) a tax exemption, (2) a tract of land limited in size and (3) a statutory condition designed to protect the interests of a spouse and lineal descendants.
Household:	One individual, or a group of individuals, living in one dwelling unit.
Hypothecate:	To pledge real of personal property as security for a debt or obligation without giving up possession of the property.
Immune Property:	Real property owned by a unit of government that is not subject to taxation.
Implied:	Expressed indirectly (e.g., an implied contract).
Implied contract:	An agreement wherein the terms are not stated but are inferred from the conduct of the parties.
Improvement:	Addition that increases the value of real property (not repairs). Buildings or other structures which become part of the land are known as improvements.
Income:	Amount earned or gained, not return of capital.
Income Approach:	An analysis used in making an appraisal in which the estimated income from the subject property is used as a basis for estimating its value.
Income Capitalization Approach:	A method for estimating the market value of a property based on the present and future income the property can be expected to generate.
Income property:	Real estate which generates a profit, such as apartments, commercial and industrial properties.
Income verification:	The act of a potential creditor to call an applicant's employer to confirm employment status and salary.
Increment earned:	An increase in value to real property due to a natural event. For example, accretion makes the parcel of property larger.
Indenture:	A contract.

CHAPTER 19 General Glossary Real Estate Terms

Industrial Revenue Bond (IRB) Type of municipal bond used for raising funds for construction of buildings to stimulate economic activity in a locality, which is exempt from federal taxation.

Ineffective (ineffectual): Status of a license when suspended. Informal proceeding A meeting at an early stage in the complaint process whereby a licensee (respondent) has an opportunity to show compliance.

Injunction: A writ or order by a court forbidding a party from doing something.

In-migration: Movement into a community or region by new residents.

Installment loan: A loan that must be repaid in no less than two payments. When establishing credit, a loan of six months or greater is preferable.

Installment Sale: A sale which, or income tax purposes, is not taxed totally in the first year of the sale. To be valid, there must be minimum of two installment payments over two tax years.

Instrument: A legal document. Insurance (See Hazard insurance.)

Insurance clause: A provision in a mortgage that required the mortgagor to obtain and keep current a hazard insurance policy.

Intangible Asset: Something of value lacking physical substance; existing only in connection with something else (e.g., the goodwill of a business).

Intangible Tax On Mortgages: State tax required prior to a mortgage being recorded. The cost is based on the face value of the mortgage.

Intensity: The concentration of activity (pedestrian and vehicular traffic) used as a means of designating land for commercial zones.

Interest: The price paid for the use of borrowed money; estate.

Interest-Only Loan: A loan for which here is no principal reduction for the full term of the loan. Payments made are interest only and the entire principle will be due at the end of the term.

Interest Rate: The percentage charged for the use of borrowed money.

Intermediation: The process whereby financial middlemen consolidate many small savings accounts belonging to individual depositors and invest those funds in large, diversified projects.

Intermingle: (See Commingle.)

Internal rate of return (IRR): A rate of discount at which the present value of future cash flows and cash reversions is equal to the initial investment.

Interpleader: A course of action when two contesting parties cannot reach an arbitrated agreement.

CHAPTER 19 General Glossary Real Estate Terms

Interval ownership	Fee simple possession, for the limited time purchased (one or more weeks), of a time-share unit, complete with deed, title and equity.
Intestate:	Without a will.
Investment:	The outlay of money in anticipation of income or profit; the sum risked, or the property purchased.
Investment contract:	A type of security using the sale of real property as the investment.
Involuntary Lien:	(involuntary alienation) A claim imposed against real property without the consent of the owner (e.g., taxes, special assessments).
Joint Tenancy:	An estate or interest owned by more than one person, each having equal rights to possession and enjoyment; the interest a deceased tenant conveys to surviving tenants by specific work=ding in the deed establishing the joint tenancy.
Joint Venture:	(joint adventure) Two or more parties in an arrangement confined to only one or a limited number of business deals.
Jointly & Severally:	A legal term indicating that a contract has been entered into by two parties and the two parties are not only liable together, but liable individually as well.
Judgment:	Decree of a court that not only declared that one party owes another party a debt but also fixes the debt amount.
Judicial Review:	The power of a court to reexamine statues or administrative acts and to determine their validity; a rehearing or appeal to a higher court.
Junior Lien:	A mortgage or other encumbrance with a secondary interest. Alien junior to another mortgage or lien.
Junior Position:	A mortgage or debt obligation that does not have the highest priority to be paid in the event of a bankruptcy. A second mortgage is a good example of a junior lien
Just Value:	The fair market t value.
Laissez-Fair:	Allow to act; noninterference by government in trade, industry and individual action generally.
Land contract:	(See Contract for Deed.)
Land Description:	(legal description) A definite and positive written identification of a specific parcel of land and its location without additional real testimony.
Land Development Loan:	Type of loan used for purchasing and or installing streets and utilities of unimproved land. Usually secured by a first mortgage and written for up to three years.
Lay Member:	One not belonging to or connected with a particular profession.
Lease:	An estate for years; an agreement that does not convey ownership but does convey possession and use for a period of time and for compensation.

CHAPTER 19 General Glossary Real Estate Terms

Leasehold:	An estate in real property held under a lease arrangement for a definite number of years; no freehold estate.
Legal Description:	A means of identifying the exact boundaries of a property. A surveyor will use the recorded plats method, metes and bounds method, or the government survey method to describe real property.
Lease Option:	An agreement between two parties where the party who owns the property extends, to the second party, the right to purchase the property at a future date. The second party lives in the property until the lease option expires.
Legal description:	A means of identifying the exact boundaries of a property. Use of the recorded plats method, metes and bound method, or the government survey method to describe real property.
Lessee:	A tenant or leaseholder; party give a lease. Lessor The landlord or owner; party granting a lease.
Level-Payment Plan:	A method for amortizing a mortgage whereby the borrower pays the same amount each month.
Leverage:	The use of borrowed funds to finance the purchase of an asset; the use of another's money to make more money.
Liability:	Debt; financial obligation; drawback/
License:	A privilege granted by the state to operate as a real estate broker, broker-salesperson or salesperson; a type of time-share interest.
Licensee:	An individual who has qualified for, and been registered as, a real estate broker, broker-salesperson or salesperson.
Licensure:	Certification as a licensee; the granting by the state of a license to practice real estate.
Lien:	A claim on property for payment of some obligation or debt.
Lienee:	One whose property is subject to a claim or charge by another.
Lienor:	One who has a claim or charge on the property of another.
Lien Theory:	Legal concept that regards a mortgage as a just claim on specific property pledged as security for a mortgage debt.
Life Estate:	A tenancy whose duration is limited to the life of some person; freehold estate.
Limited Partnership:	A business entity consisting of one or more general partners and one or more limited partner.
Line of Credit:	The amount of money that a lender makes available to a borrower.
Lineal:	Descended in a direct family line; relating to or derived from ancestors.
Liquidated Damages:	The amount of valuable consideration specified in an agreement as a penalty for default (*see also* Damages).

CHAPTER 19 General Glossary Real Estate Terms

Liquidation: The process of determining liabilities and apportioning the assets in order to discharge the indebtedness of a business to be sold.

Liquidity: The ability to convert none-cash assets into cash quickly, refers to a firm's cash position and its ability to meet obligations.

Lis Pendens: A pending legal action.

Listing: Oral or written employment agreement between a broker (or a salesperson employed by a broker) and the property owner; authorization to sell, rent or exchange.

Litigation: A lawsuit; the act of carrying on a lawsuit; a case before the court of law.

Littoral Legal rights related to land abutting an ocean, sea or lake, usually extending to the high-water mark.

Loan application Information form filled out by borrower for the lender to base his decision on the making of a loan

Loan Closing: Executed by a loan officer authorizing the signing of the loan agreement and issuance of funds.

Loan Commitment: A pledge made by the lender which states the terms and conditions to be met to make a loan.

Loan Correspondent: Generally, a mortgage banker or company that provides services for lending institutions.

Loan Fee: A fee over and above the annual interest the lender charges the borrower for making a loan.

Loan-to-value(L/V) ratio: Relationship between amount borrowed and appraised value (or sales price) of a property. Lock-in clause A condition in a mortgage that keeps the borrower from paying off the loan before the specified time.

Lot and Block Number: A Type of legal description of land.

M.A.I.: A person who is a member of the American Institute of Real Estate Appraisers of the National Association of Realtors.

Maintenance Clause: A provision in a mortgage agreement that required mortgagors (borrowers) to maintain mortgaged property in good condition.

Majority: A person having attained 18 years of age, or having married or by court order; no longer a minor; a number greater than half the total.

Malfeasance: The committing of an unlawful act, especially by a public official.

Mandamus, (writ of): An order of a superior court directing a lower court or body to do some specified act.

Mandate: Directive from a higher authority to a lower body.

Marketable Title (merchantable title): Rights to real property that are so clear that a buyer may have peaceful and quiet enjoyment of the property free of litigation.

Market Value: The most probable price a property will bring from a fully informed buyer, willing but not compelled to buy, and the lowest price a fully informed seller will accept if not compelled to sell.

CHAPTER 19 General Glossary Real Estate Terms

Master in Chancery:	An appointed assistant to a court.
Mechanic's Lien:	A claim based on the principle of "unjust enrichment"; favors parties who have performed labor or delivered material or supplies for the repair or construction of an improvement to real property.
Mediation:	The act of having a third-party attempt to reconcile a dispute between two parties.
Meeting of the Minds:	The point when two people, thinking of the same thing, reach an agreement through an offer and acceptance.
Meridian:	Any of the imaginary lines of longitude on the earth's surface; in land description, the vertical lines running in a north-south direction parallel to the principal (prime) meridian and separating the various ranges.
Metes and Bounds:	A type of land description ("metes" means measurements and "bounds" mean boundaries).
Middleman:	An intermediary who merely brings two parties together.
Mill:	A unit of money used to specify a property tax rate ($1 for each $1,000 of taxable value).
Millage:	A tax rate, expressed as the number of mills to be applied.
Misdemeanor:	Any crime punishable by fine or imprisonment other than in a penitentiary.
Misfeasance:	A lawful act done in a negligent or unlawful manner.
Misrepresentation:	A false or misleading statement of a material fact; concealment of a material fact.
Modified Accelerated Cost Recovery System (MACRS):	The current methods of determining the depreciation allowed for income tax purposes on real property.
Monuments:	A type of land description using physical features of the land.
Moral Turpitude:	An act of corruption, vileness or moral depravity; a disgraceful action or deed.
Mortgage:	A written agreement that pledges property as security for payment of a debt.
Mortgage Banker:	One who makes mortgage loans with the expectation of reselling them to an institutional lender. Mortgage broker One who finds a mortgage lender for a potential borrower, and vice versa.
Mortgagee:	A lender who holds a mortgage on specific property as security for the money loaned to the borrower. Mortgage insurance premiums (MIPs) Fees paid by FHA borrowers to obtain a loan (up front and annual).
Mortgagor:	A borrower who gives a mortgage on his or her property in order to obtain a loan from a lender.
Multiple Licenses:	Licenses held by a broker in two or more real estate brokerage firms.

CHAPTER 19 General Glossary Real Estate Terms

Multiple Listing Service (MLS): An arrangement among members of a real estate board or exchange that allows each member broker to share listings with other members so that greater exposure is obtained, and greater chance of sale will result.

Negative Amortization: A financing arrangement whereby monthly mortgage payments are less than required to pay both interest and principal. The unpaid amount is added to the loan balance.

Net Income: Profit from property or business after expenses have been deducted; effective gross income less operating expenses.

Net Lease: An arrangement in which the lessee pays all operating expenses and real estate taxes in addition to paying rent.

Net Listing: An agreement or contract to sell or rent a property for a specified minimum net amount for the owner.

Net Operating Income (NOI): The resulting amount when all operating expenses are subtracted from effective gross income.

Net Present Value (NPV): A method or ranking investment proposals.

Nolo Contendere: A pleading of no contest by a defendant; a plea in a criminal action not admitting guilt but subjecting the defendant to punishment as if it were a guilty plea.

Nonconforming Use: Continuing land use that is not in compliance with zoning ordinances.

Nonfreehold Estate (leasehold interest): An estate in real property in which ownership is for a determinable time period, as in a lease.

Note: Legal evidence of a debt that must accompany a mortgage in Florida; a legally executed pledge to pay a stipulated sum of money (see also Promissory note).

Notice (See Actual and Constructive notice.)

Novation: The substitution of a new party and/or new terms to an existing obligation.

Obligee: A lender or mortgagee. Obligor A borrower or mortgagor.

Obsolescence: Any loss in value (see also Depreciation). Offer An intentional proposal or promise made by one party to act or perform provided the other party acts or performs in the manner requested.

Offeree: One who receives an offer, usually the seller. Offeror One who makes an offer, usually the buyer.

Open-end clause: A provision in a mortgage allowing the borrower to increase he loan amount as long as the total debt does not exceed the original mortgage loan amount, with the lender often reserving the right to adjust the interest rate to current market rates; a mortgage for future advances.

CHAPTER 19 General Glossary Real Estate Terms

Open Listing: A listing given to any number of brokers who work simultaneously to sell the owner's property.

Operating Expense Ratio: The relationship between operating expenses and effective gross income.

Opinion of Title: A formal statement by an attorney regarding the status of a title after examination of the chain of title.

Opinion of Value: An estimate of a property's worth given by a li8censee for the purpose of a prospective sale.

Option: A right or privilege to purchase or lease real property at a specified price during a designated period based on a sufficient consideration.

Optionee: The party who takes an option and pays a consideration.

Optionor: The party who gives an option and receives a consideration.

Oral Contract: An agreement that is not in writing.

Origination Fee: A charge by a lender for taking a mortgage in exchange for a loan.

Ostensible Partnership (quasi-partnership: One or more parties cause a third party to be deceived into believing that a partnership exists when no such arrangement exists.

Outstanding balance: Amount of a loan that has not yet been repaid.

Overage (secret profit; secret commission): Retaining more than the agreed amount or sales commission, without the express knowledge and consent of the parties involved; a form of fraud.

Overall Capitalization rate (OCR): The relationship between annual net operating income and the value or sales price of a property.

Overdraft Protection: An extra service that most financial institutions offer their checking account customers. Much like a credit card, in that if the client writes check for an amount greater than what is in the checking account, the bank automatically writes the client a "loan." Interest and annual fee may be charged against this loan.

Over improvement: An addition or change to property not in line with its highest and best use, or a betterment that exceeds that justified by local conditions.

Package Mortgage: A loan covering both real and personal property.

Partial Release Clause: A clause in a trust deed that allows for reconveyance of title of part of the property when a part of the loan is paid off.

Participation: On some mortgage loans on income property, a small percentage of the gross income is required addition to the interest.

Partnership: Two or more competent individuals each of whom agrees to share in the profits and losses of the business.

Pass-through securities: Certificates pledging a group (pool) of existing government-backed mortgages used for the purpose of channeling funds into housing market.

Payoff Period: The time in which a loan must be paid off in full.

Penalty Clause: A provision in a mortgage that required the borrower to pay a penalty in money if the mortgage payments are made in advance of the normal due date or if the mortgage is paid in full ahead of schedule.

Pension Fund: An employee retirement reserve used as a source of permanent financing for real estate.

Per Diem: By the day; per day; an allowance for daily expenses.

Performance: Point when a party or parties to a contract fulfill the promises or obligations in the contract.

Permanent Mortgage: Same as a long-term loan, usually five years or more.

Personal Property (personalty; chattel): Tangible and movable property (transferred by bill of sale) property not classified as real property.

Personal Representative: Executor or administrator of a deceased person's estate.

Personality: (See Personal property.)

Petition for Review: A request to a court of appeal (appellate court) asking it to examine the record of the proceedings in a specific case (see also Judicial review).

Plaintiff: The person or party bringing suit or charges; the complaining party; complainant.

Planned unit development (PUD): A residential project with mixed land uses and high residential density.

Planning: Devising ways and means for achieving desired goals.

Planning Commission: An official agency, usually made up of appointed lay citizens, that directs and con- trols the use, design and development of land in a city, county or region.

Plat (plat map): A plan of a tract of land subdivided into lots and showing required or planned amenities.

Point of beginning (POB): The starting (and ending) place in a land survey using the metes and bounds method of property description.

Points A percentage of the loan amount paid to the lender when the loan is negotiated for the privilege of borrowing a sum of money. Each point is one percent.

Police powers: The authority of government to protect the property, life, health and welfare of its citizens.

Policy manual: The notebook of written rules and regulations that set desired standards and procedures in an office.

Portfolio: A collection of securities and other investments held by a person or company.

CHAPTER 19 General Glossary Real Estate Terms

Potential Gross Income: The total annual income a property would produce with 100 percent occupancy and no collection or vacancy losses.

Power of Attorney: (See Attorney, power of.)

Preliminary Title Search: The first review of all previously recorded documents regarding a specific property, to make sure that the property may be sold.

Premises Clause: (See Granting clause.)

Premium: An additional sum of money paid as an incentive to induce someone to do something.

Prepayment Clause: A provision in a mortgage that allows the mortgagor to pay the mortgage debt ahead of schedule without penalty.

Prescription, Easement By: A method of acquiring an interest in real property through long and continued use.

Present Value: The worth of all future benefits of an investment in terms of today's dollars.

Price: The amount paid for something.

Prima Facie Evidence: Requiring no further proof; acceptable on the face of.

Primary Lender: Financial institution that makes mortgage loans directly to borrowers (e.g., savings and loans, banks). Primary market A source for the purchase of a mortgage loan by a borrower.

Prime Rate: The interest rates on bank loans regarded as the rate commercial banks will charge their top borrowers at a particular time.

Principal: The party employing the services of a real estate broker; amount of money borrowed in a mortgage loan, excluding interest and other charges.

Principal (prime) meridian: An imaginary line running north and south and crossing a base line at a definite point; used by surveyors for reference in locating and describing land under the government survey systems

Private mortgage insurance (PMI): Needed to insure all of the mortgage representing more than 80 percent of appraised value or purchase price.

Probable Cause: Reasonable grounds or justification for prosecuting.

Probation: A suspended sentence during good behavior, usually under supervision.

Proceeds: The profits derived from investing.

Procuring Cause: The person whose efforts are the cause of an executed sales contract, regardless of who actually writes the contract.

Professional Association (P.A.): A business corporation consisting of one or more individuals engaged in a primary business that provides a professional service (e.g., lawyer, doctor).

Proforma Statement: An estimate of the economic results of a proposed project; a projected income statement.

Promissory note: A written promise to pay a specific amount (see also Note).

CHAPTER 19 General Glossary Real Estate Terms

NOTES:

Property: A bundle of legal rights.

Property Insurance: (See Hazard insurance.)

Property Management: One of the component activities of the agency division of the real estate business.

Proprietary Lease: A written agreement between the owner/corporation and the tenant/stockholder in a cooperative apartment.

Prorate: To divide or assess proportionate shares of charges and credits between the buyer and the seller according to their individual period of ownership.

Prospect: The customer with whom a licensee hopes to be successful in accomplishing the purpose of employment.

Proxy: A document that allows one person to act for another.

Purchase-Money Mortgage (purchase money): Any new mortgage taken as part of the purchase price of real property by the seller.

Quadrant: Quarter; any of the four quarters into which something is divided.

Qualification: The process of reviewing prior to approval (of a buyers' housing needs and financial abilities, of a borrower's mortgage loan application or of an application for licensure) (See also Underwriting).

Quasi: As if; of a similar nature; seemingly.

Quasi-judicial power: FREC Duties related to the granting, denying, suspending and revoking of licenses.

Quasi-legislative power: FREC Duties related to the creation of rules and regulations.

Quasi-partnership: (See Ostensible partnership.)

Quiet Enjoyment: A provision in a deed guaranteeing that the buyer may enjoy possession of the property in peace and without disturbance by reason of other claims on the title by the seller or anyone else.

Quiet Title: A suit or action in a court to remove a defect, cloud or claim against the title to real property.

Quitclaim Deed: A type of deed that will effectively convey any present interest, claim or title to real property that the seller (grantor) may own.

Quorum: The minimum number of persons who may lawfully transact the business of a meeting (51 percent or four of the members of the Florida Real Estate Commission). Range In the government survey system of land description, a vertical strip of land six miles wide located between two consecutive sub meridians or range lines.

Rapport: A good relationship full of trust.

Range lines (submeridians): The surveyed north-south lines running every six miles east and west of the principal meridian

Rate of Return: The amount of profit, usually expressed as a percentage, one receives compared to the amount of money invested.

Ratio: The relationship in quantity, size or amount between two things; proportion.

CHAPTER 19 General Glossary Real Estate Terms

NOTES:

Ready, Willing and Able: "Ready" indicates the prospect is in a position and of a mind to complete the transaction: "willing" implies that the prospect desires to do so at the price and terms agree; "able" refers to the prospect's financial ability to produce the required money when necessary.

Real Estate: Land, including the air above and the earth below plus any permanent improvements affecting the utility of the land; real property; property that is not personal property.

Real Estate Agent: A salesperson associated with a broker, who acts in behalf of a broker.

Recording: The act of entering in the public record, any instrument effecting title to real property.

Real Estate Business: A commercial activity in which the sale, purchase, leasing, rental, exchange or management of real property is conducted by qualified and licensed parties acting either for themselves or for others for compensation.

R.E.O. (Real Estate owned): Properties that financial institutions have repossessed as a result of a default on a mortgage and which these institutions are willing to sell. Real estate profession Actually, still a semiprofessional requiring knowledge of real estate values, experience in dealing with the public, plus exceptional personal integrity and character as qualifications to act as advisors and agents for members of the public.

Real Property: Any interest or estate in land, including leaseholds, sub leaseholds, business opportunities and enterprises and mineral rights, real estate.

Realtor®: A real estate broker who is a member of a local board of Realtors® and is affiliated with the state association (Florida Association of Realtors®) and the National Association of Realtors* (not synonymous with "Real Estate Agent").

Realty: A synonym for real estate and real property. Reasonable time A variable period of time, which may be affected by market conditions, desires of the owner, supply and demand, fluctuations of values or an official decision.

Receivables: Money or notes due to a business from other. Receivership clause A provision in a mortgage, related to income-producing property, that is designed to require that income derived shall be used to make mortgage payments in the event the mortgagor (borrower) defaults. Recommended order A determination by a hearing officer that includes findings and conclusions as well as other information required by law or agency rule to be in a final order.

Record: As a verb, to place any document or instrument affecting title or an interest in real property in the public records of the county in which the property is located.

CHAPTER 19 General Glossary Real Estate Terms

Reconveyance: The transfer of title of land from one person to the immediately preceding owner, commonly used when a debt is satisfied.

Recovery Fund (Real Estate Recovery Fund): A state regulated account to cover claims of aggrieved parties who have suffered monetary losses from licensees' actions.

Recovery Period: The assigned time over which property is depreciated for tax purposes.

Rectangular Method: (See Government loaned survey system).

Reddendum Clause: (reserving clause) A provision in a deed to reserve some right or restriction for the grantor (seller).

Redemption: To repurchase, to buy back, to recover property used as security for a mortgage by paying the debt (see also Equity of redemption).

Refinance: To pay off an existing debt with the proceeds of another.

Redlining: Discriminatory financing by a lending institution registration Authorization by the state to place an applicant on the register(record) of officially recognized individuals and businesses.

Release Clause: A provision in a blanket mortgage covering more than one unit or real property that provides for the mortgagor to obtain freedom from the mortgage for each unit when a designated amount has been paid to the mortgagee for each unit.

Reliction: Gradual receding of water and resulting permanent increase in land once covered.

Remainderman: The party designated to receive a remainder estate. Two types: vested remainderman (one who is known and named) and contingent remainderman (one whose identity is not certain or one to be selected).

Rent Control: The regulation or restrictions set by government agencies on the amount of rent that landlords may charge.

Repossession: The act whereby the lender reclaims durable goods bought on credit when the payments are past due.

Renunciation: To abandon an acquired right without transferring that right to another.

Replacement reserves (reserve for replacements): A portion of the annual income set aside for covering the cost of major components (e.g., air-conditioning) that wear out faster than the building itself.

Reprimand: An official act of oral and/or written criticism with a formal warning included.

Reproduction Cost: Amount required to duplicate the property exactly.

Rescind: To annul, cancel, repeal or terminate. Reserve for replacements (See Replacement reserves.)

CHAPTER 19 General Glossary Real Estate Terms

Respondent: A person who answers to an informal complaint proceeding prior to being adjudged innocent or being named as a defendant.

Restriction: Any device or action that controls or limits the use of real property.

Reversion: That portion of the net proceeds from the sale of property that represents the return of the investor's capital.

Revocation: To cancel, rescind, annul or make void; the permanent cancelation of a person's license.

Right-To-Use: A leasehold interest in a time-share unit based on the limited time (one or more weeks) specified in the agreement.

Riparian Rights: Private ownership rights extending to the normal high-water mark along a river or stream and including access rights to water, boating, bathing and dockage in accordance with state and federal statutes.

Risk: The chance of loss of all or part of an investment; the uncertainty of financial loss.

Sale and leaseback: A financing arrangement in which an investor buys property owned and used by a business accompanied by a simultaneous leasing back of the property to the business by the buyer/investor.

Sales contract: Deposit receipt contract; purchase agreement; contract for sale and purchase) An agreement whereby one party agrees to sell, and the other party agrees to buy according to the terms set forth.

Salesperson: A licensed individual who, for compensation, is employed by a broker or owner/developer.

Sandwich lease: While having the option to buy a proper- ty, the investor subleases it to gain a positive cash flow.

Satisfaction of Mortgage: An instrument filed in the public records, which acknowledges payment of an indebtedness secured by a mortgage.

Savings Association Insurance Fund (SAIF): A federal agency that insures deposits of member S&Ls.

Seal: A mark, emblem or impression on a document used to authenticate the document or a signature.

Secondary Market: A source for the purchase and sale of existing mortgages.

Second Mortgage (secondary financing): A loan that is junior or subordinate to a first mortgage, normally taken out when the borrower needs more money.

Secret Profit or Commission: *(See Overage.)*

Section: One of the primary units of measurement in the government survey system of land description. A section is one mile square and contains 640 acres.

Security: The collateral that the borrower puts up to guarantee repayment of the loan.

CHAPTER 19 General Glossary Real Estate Terms

Security Deposit:	An amount of money paid by a tenant before moving into the premises to cover any damage incurred while living there or unpaid rent in the event the tenant leaves without notice.
Security Interest:	The interest that the lender has in the collateral of a loan to assure repayment.
Secured Note:	A note that has a provision that certain pledged property may be claimed by the lender as payment of a debt upon its default.
Seisin(seizin)clause:	A covenant in a deed that warrants that the grantor (seller) holds the property by virtue of a fee simple title and has a complete right to dispose of same.
Seller's market:	The demand for available properties exceeds the supply.
Separate Property:	Real property owned by a husband or wife prior to the marriage with the spouse having no present rights in such property; property owned individually.
Service (secondary) industry:	A business that attracts local money (e.g., grocery store, retail shop).
Setback:	Restrictions established by zoning or deed on the space required between lot lines and building lines.
Severalty:	Sole ownership of real property ("severed" from all other).
Severance:	The act of removing something attached to the land (e.g., fruit, timber, fence).
Servicing a Debt:	The act of paying the annual principal and interest payments on an outstanding debt obligation. Short term Most short-term loans are two or less years in length.
Site Plan:	A document that indicates the improvement details for a project of greater-than-average size.
Situs (location):	Relationships and influences created by location of property, which affect value (e.g., accessibility, personal preference).
Sole Proprietorship:	Dealing as an individual in business. Special assessment A tax levied against property to pay for all, or part of, an improvement that will benefit the property being assessed.
Special Exception:	An individual ruling in which a property owner is granted the right to use otherwise contrary to law. Specific lien A claim that affects only the property designated in the lien instrument or agreement.
Specific Performance:	A remedy for an injured party obtained through a court of equity, which requires specific accomplishment of the contract terms by a defendant.
Standby Commitment:	A promise made by lender to stand by to fund a mortgage loan that he does not expect to fund unless the project gets into trouble. Used by a developer to get a construction loan.
State-Certified Appraiser:	A person verified by the DBPR as qualified to issue state-certified real property appraisals.

CHAPTER 19 General Glossary Real Estate Terms

Statute:	An established rule or law passed by a legislative body.
Statute of frauds:	An act that requires that certain real estate instruments and contracts affecting title to real property be in writing in order to be enforceable.
Statute of limitations:	An act that prescribes specific time restrictions for enforcement of rights by action of law.
Stay:	Delay temporarily; stop for a limited time. Steering Discriminatory acts against buyers.
Stock:	The ownership element in a corporation usually divided into shares and represented by transferrable certificates (may be divided into two or more classes of differing rights and stated values).
Sub baselines:	(See Township lines.)
Subcontractors:	A third party who assumes the responsibility and obligations of a second party's contract through assignment.
Subdivide:	To segment large, acquired tracts of real property in order to create small tracts for the purpose of resale.
Subject Property:	The real property under discussion or appraisal.
Subject to the mortgage	A buyer makes regular periodic payments on the mortgage but does not assume responsibility for the mortgage.
Sublease:	A lessee leasing a property to a third party for a period of time less than the original lease (also referred to as subletting).
Submeridians:	(See Range lines.)
Subordination:	Made subject to or subservient to; assignment to a lesser role or position.
Subordination clause:	A provision in a mortgage in which the lender voluntarily permits a prior or subsequent mortgage to take priority over the lender's otherwise superior mortgage; the act of yielding priority.
Subpoena:	A writ or order commanding the person named to appear and testify in a legal proceeding.
Subrogation:	(See Subordination.)
Substitution, Principle of:	An economic law of value: not prudent buyer will pay more for a property than the cost of an equally desirable replacement property.
Suit:	An act of suing; an action in a court of law for the recovery of a right or claim.
Summary Suspension:	Emergency or immediate suspension of a license to protect the public.
Supersedeas, Writ of:	A stay of enforcement; temporary stop in a legal proceeding; restraining order.
Supply (principle of supply and demand):	The quantity of goods or services offered for sale to consumers.
Survey:	The procedure used to measure and describe a specific tract of real property for the purpose of deter- mining exact boundaries and the area contained therein.

CHAPTER 19 General Glossary Real Estate Terms

Survivorship, Right of: A legal concept whereby the surviving owners of a joint interest in real property are entitle to the interest formerly owned by one or more deceased owners.

Suspension: To cause to cease operating for a period of time; the temporary withholding of a person's license rendering it ineffective; a period of enforce inactivity.

Syndicate: (See Business trust.)

Tandem Plan: A method used to accomplish GNMA's special assistance goals in cooperation with FNMA. Tangible asset Anything of substance; personal and real property (e.g., cash, building, equipment, land).

Tax: Compulsory payment paid by a citizen to a unit of government.

Tax deductible: An item that is not taxed.

Tax liability: The amount of money one owes to the government for taxation purposes.

Taxable income: Gross income minus tax deductions; net operating income plus reserve for replacements minus financing costs and allowable depreciation.

Taxable value: The assessed value less allowable exemptions resulting in an amount to which the tax rate is applied to determine property taxes due.

Tax certificate: A document sold by a local tax authority granting the certificate buyer the right to receive delinquent taxes plus interest when paid by the legal property owner.

Tax clause: A provision in a mortgage that requires the borrower to pay all legitimate property taxes.

Tax deed: A type of deed used to convey title after real property is sold at auction by public authority for nonpayment of taxes.

Tax district: An authority, such as a city, county, school boards or special levy area (e.g., water district), with the power to assess property owners annually in order to meet its expenditures for the public good.

Tax lien: A claim against real property arising out of nonpayment of the property taxes.

Tax rate: The percentage of value that is used to determine the amount of tax to be levied against each individual unit of property; ad valorem (according to the value).

Tax shelter: An investment that shields items of income or gain from payment of income taxes; a term used to describe some tax advantages of owning real property (or their investment), including postponement or even elimination of certain taxes.

Tenancy: The estate or rights of a tenant (see also Estate).

Tenancy at Sufferance: An estate lawfully acquired for a temporary period of time but retained after a period of lawful possession has expired; nonfreehold estate.

CHAPTER 19 General Glossary Real Estate Terms

Tenancy at Will:	An estate that may be terminated by either party at any time upon proper notice; nonfreehold estate.
Tenancy By The Entireties (See Estate by the entireties.):	Tenancy in common A form o9f ownership by two or more persons each having an equal or unequal interest and passing the interest to heirs, not to surviving tenants.
Tenant:	A person or party with rights of occupancy or possession of real property.
Tenendum Clause:	Provision in a deed designed to specify those improvements or other rights that are being transferred in addition to the land itself.
Term Loan:	A nonamortizing mortgage that normally calls for repayment of the principal in full at the end of the loan term (see also Balloon mortgage.)
Testate:	Having left a will.
Testator (testatrix):	A person who makes a will.
Third Party:	Generally, a member of the public; not the principal or agent in a transaction.
Tier (township):	An east-west row of townships (as used in the government survey method of land description).
Time Is Of The Essence:	A phrase in a contract making failure to perform by a specified date a breach or violation of the agreement.
Time-share:	An individual interest in a real property unit together with a right of exclusive use for a specified number of days or weeks per year.
Title:	The group of rights that represent ownership of real property and the quality of the estate owned; evidence of ownership of property; legal title.
Title insurance:	A policy of insurance that protects the holder from any loss resulting from defects in the title.
Title Plant:	Copies of recorded documents from the public records kept by title insurance companies; record room.
Title Search:	A check of public records, usually done by a title office, to determine current
Title Theory:	Legal concept that vests title to mortgaged property in the mortgagee(lender) or third party.
Topography:	Surface features (natural and man-made) of land (e.g., lakes, mountains, roads).
Township:	A square tract of land measuring six miles on each side and including 36 sections (formed by the crossing of range and township lines).
Township lines (subaselines):	The east-west survey lines located every six miles north and south of the primary base line.
Trade Name:	Any adopted of fictitious name used to designate a business concern.
Trust:	A right of property, either real or personal, held by one party for the benefit of another.
Trust account:	(See Escrow account.)

CHAPTER 19 General Glossary Real Estate Terms

Trustee (escrow agent): A person or party, either appointed or required by law to administer or manage another's property.

Trust Deed: Deed given by borrower to beneficiary to be held pending fulfillment of an obligation, which is ordinarily repayment of a loan to a beneficiary.

Underwriting (loan qualification; risk analysis): The analysis of the extent of risk assumed by a lender in connection with a proposed mortgage loan.

Unilateral contract: An agreement in which only one party promises to perform without receiving a reciprocal promise to perform from the other party.

Unincorporated association: A group of people associated together for some common, noncommercial purpose.

Unities (four unities: Individual prerequisites required to constitute a single joint tenancy.

Unliquidated damages: The amount of valuable consideration awarded by a court to an injured party as a result of default (see also Damages).

Unsecured note: A loan granted without the security of collateral on the basis of a borrower's credit worthiness and signature.

Usury: Charging a rate of interest greater than the legal one; unlawful interest.

Vacate: To set aside, cancel or annul; to leave empty. Valid Sufficient to be legally bind; enforceable.

Valid Contract: An agreement binding on both parties and legally enforceable against all parties to the agreement.

Value: The worth of something.

Variable Rate Mortgage: A loan which carriers an interest rate that is tied to a specific index and can fluctuate periodically during the term of the loan.

Variance: An exception to zoning regulations or ordinances granted to relieve a hardship.

Vendee: The buyer or purchaser of real property under an agreement of sale.

Vendor: The seller of real property in an agreement of sale. Vendor's lien A claim against property giving the seller the right to hold the property as security for any unpaid purchase money.

Verification: A sworn statement before a qualified officer to the correct content of a document.

Veterans Affairs (VA): Guarantees mortgage loans to encourage private lending agencies to give liberal mortgages to veterans and their spouses.

Venture Capital: Money invested in a new venture which is usually considered high risk.

Vested: Fixed or settled.

Void: Invalid; without force; no longer effective.

CHAPTER 19 General Glossary Real Estate Terms

Voluntary lien (voluntary alienation): A claim imposed against real property with the consent of the owner (e.g., mortgage, vendor's lien).

Warrant: A guarantee or covenant, as in a warranty deed. Warranty deed (general warranty deed) A type of deed containing the strongest and most comprehensive promises of further assurance possible for a grantor (seller) to convey to a grantee (buyer).

Warranty Forever: A provision in a deed guaranteeing that the seller will for all time warrant and defend the title and possession for the buyer.

Waste: An improper use or abuse of property by one who holds less than the fee simple ownership of it.

Will: A written document legally executed and containing the essentials of a "last will and testament" by which an individual dispose of his or her estate, effective after death.

Witness: A person who gives testimony; one who observes and attests to the signing or executing of a document.

Wraparound Mortgage: A financing technique in which the payment of the existing mortgage is continued (by the seller) and a new, higher interest rate mortgage, which is larger than the existing mortgage, is paid by the buyer/borrower.

Writ: A court order directing a party to do a specific act, usually to appear in, or report to, a court of law.

Writ of Certiorari: (see Certiorari, writ of.)

Writ of Mandamus: (see Mandamus, writ of.) Writ of supersedeas (See Supersedeas, writ of.)

Yield: The rate of return; the return on an investment or the amount of profit stated as a percentage of the amount invested; the ratio of the annual net income from a property to the cost or market value of the property.

Zoning: Classification of real property for various purposes; the government power to control and supervise the utilization of privately owned real property (actually, the exercise of police powers).

Index

Symbols
2/28 36
2mp 24
80/20 Loan 35
100% Financing 35

A
Adjustabe Rate Mortgages .... 19, 32 ,36, 98
ARM 32, 36, 62, 71, 74
Arm»s Length Transaction 75,114
Authorization to Release Information . 99, 102, 147
Avoid Foreclosure 145

B
Bank Accounts 93
Bankruptcy 90, 113
Brand Yourself 65
Broker Price Opinion 147
Borrower»s Options 57

C
Certified Expert 49
Competitive Market Analyst (CMA) . . 89, 108, 109, 110
Cost of Repair 108
Credit Rating 129

D
Deed 36, 39, 40, 136
Deed-in-Lieu of Foreclosure . 24, 25, 29, 51, 59, 133
Default 11, 19, 26, 38, 39, 40, 42, 45, 82, 85, 147, 148, 158, 176
Deficiency Judgement 10, 50, 51, 57 132, 147
Definitions 147
Disclaimer 93
Distressed Property 147
Distressed Property Market 147

E
Equator 142
Equity of Redemption 11
Exclusive Right of Sale Listing Agreement 100

F
Fair Market Value 162
Federal Tax Returns 10, 66, 82, 93
FHA 22
FHA Qualifications and Procedures 51, 52, 131
Finanical Statements 92
Forbearance 58, 147, 163
Foreclosure 10, 50, 57, 148
Foreclosure Law Citations 41, 42, 43, 44, 45
Foreclosure Timeline 108

H
HAFA 23, 24, 25, 26, 27, 28, 29, 30, 52, 90, 131
HAMP 24, 30
Hardship 58, 59, 67, 68, 69
Hardship Letter 68, 74, 78, 79, 94, 108, 116, 148
HELOCS 91, 112
Home Affordable Foreclosure Alternatives . 23, 24, 25, 26, 27, 28, 29, 30, 52, 90, 131
Home Affordable Foreclosure Alternatives Program 23, 24, 25, 26, 27, 28, 29, 30, 52, 90, 131
HOA 12, 104
Home Affordable Modification Program 24, 30
Home Equity Line of Credit
Homeowner»s Association 12, 104
HUD - 1 .... 126, 127
HUD Frequently Asked Questions 23

I
Income Stream 53, 119, 120
Insolvency 59, 69, 95
Inspection Report 108
Investor 16, 18, 26, 50, 57, 58, 59, 72, 75, 77, 95, 105, 113, 130
IRS 66, 93

J
Jump Start 83
Junior Liens 13

L
Legal Public Notice 86
Liar Loans 36
Liens 12, 13, 26, 91
Lis Pendens 11
Loan Modification 51, 57, 131

Index

M
Marketing your Listings 105, 106, 107
Mechanic»s Liens 13
Method of Foreclosure 46, 47
MLS Listing 106
Modification to Listing Agreement 100, 107
Mortgage Crisis 3, 17, 21, 84
Mortgage Electronic Registration System (MERS) . 87, 88
Mortgage Forgiveness Debt Relief Act of 2007 .145
Mortgage Modification 142
Mortgage Re-Instatement 58
Mortgage Payoff 101, 105

N
NFSSICE.com 55
NINA 36
NINJA Loans 36
No-Doc 36
No Income No Asset 36
Non-Performance Addendum 100
Notice of Action 85
Notice of Sale 11, 85, 148

O
Offer is Accepted 111, 112, 113, 114, 115

P
Paycheck Stubs 93
PMI 174
Preliminary HUD 78, 112
Price Changes 157
Problems to Avoid 122
Proof of Income 93

R
Redemption Period 10
Reinstatement 58, 59
REO Property 106, 108, 142, 148

S
Savings and Loan Crisis 14, 15, 161
Security Clearances 91
Security Devices 38, 39
Sellers Package 65, 92
Servicemembers Civil Relief Act (SCRAM) . 61, 97
Short Sale 25, 51, 59, 69, 129, 149
Short Sale Addendum 100
Short Sale Definitions 147
Short Sale Package 116
Short Pay 148
Showing Appointments Log 111
Submitting the Lender / Investor Package 116
Sub-Prime Lending ..17, 18, 19, 20, 21, 33, 59, 61, 62, 69, 95, 96, 98
Sub-Prime Loans . . 17, 18, 19, 20, 21, 33, 59, 61, 62, 69, 95, 96, 98
Summary Final Judgement 12

T
Tax Consequences 28
Title Insurance 137, 139, 140
Title Search 104, 112

U
Underwater 149

W
WholesaleProperties.com 52, 53, 106

Y
Yield Spread Premium 33

NOTES

www.ingramcontent.com/pod-product-compliance
Lightning Source LLC
Chambersburg PA
CBHW080505110426
42742CB00017B/3006